M AX

SEAS
OF THE WORLD

A *GUIDE TO THE BETTER-KNOWN SPECIES*

by
R. TUCKER ABBOTT, Ph.D.
Du Pont Chair of Malacology
Delaware Museum of Natural History

Under the editorship of
HERBERT S. ZIM, Ph.D., Sc.D.

Illustrated by
GEORGE AND MARITA SANDSTRÖM

Imperial Harp   3"
Indian Ocean
Harpa costata L.

 GOLDEN PRESS • NEW YORK
Western Publishing Company, Inc.
Racine, Wisconsin

FOREWORD

Shells occupy a unique place in the natural world. No other animals are as widely collected, traded, or bought and sold because of their beauty, attractiveness and rarity. Each year an increasing number of people want to identify, classify and understand the beautiful shells they see or collect. This guide is necessarily a brief sampling of the many thousands of marine shells. Because it is a guide for collecting we have emphasized attractive and better-known species, occasionally slighting some common species and familiar genera. We hope that the pastime of shell collecting will lead to increasing interest in the fascinating animals which make the shells.

The author, editor and artists wish to express their appreciation to the Academy of Natural Sciences of Philadelphia for the use of its extensive research collections in the preparation of this book. We also owe a debt to the artists, George and Marita Sandström, for their excellent work on the illustrations.

R.T.A.
H.S.Z.

Carrier Shell (*Xenophora*) is the original shell collector. It gathers small empty shells and attaches them to itself. This is the common **Japanese Carrier Shell**.

THE CLASSES OF MOLLUSKS

All seashells have soft bodies. The thin, fleshy mantle usually secretes a limy shell, either as a single cone or a pair of valves, or rarely in 8 parts. About half the mollusks are marine; the others land or fresh-water.

Marine   Fresh-water   Land

SNAILS, or Gastropods, have a single shell, usually coiled. They have a distinct head with tentacles and a rasping tongue (the radula). Most of the 80,000 species have shells. (pp. 22-128)

pp. 129-155

BIVALVES, or Pelecypods, are mollusks with two valves joined by a hinge, a horny ligament, and one or two muscles. Most of the 10,000 species are marine; others are fresh-water.

CEPHALOPODS include squid, octopus and the Nautilus. Very active animals with large eyes, powerful jaws and with 8-90 tentacles. About 800 species.

TUSK SHELLS (about 200 marine species) live in curved, tooth-like shells open at both ends.

p. 7

pp. 156-157

CHITONS are primitive, marine mollusks with 8-plated shells imbedded in tough tissue. There are about 600 shallow-water species.

p. 7

MONOPLACOPHORA until recently known only from fossils. A rare deep-sea, primitive group. The soft parts are segmented. 1"

Frog Shells
page 67

Tritons
page 68

Tuns
page 70

Bubble
Shells
page 128

Order
TECTIBRANCHIA

Moon Snails
page 49

Helmets
page 63

Cowries
page 51

True Conchs
page 42

Ceriths
page 39

Sundials
page 38

Wentletraps
page 40

Slipper Shells
page 41

Order
MESOGASTROPODA

Nerites
page 36

Periwinkles
page 37

Top Shells
page 28

Turbans
page 32

True
Limpets
page 27

Keyhole Limpets
page 26

Order
ARCHAEGASTROPODA

Abalones
page 24

Slit Shells
page 23

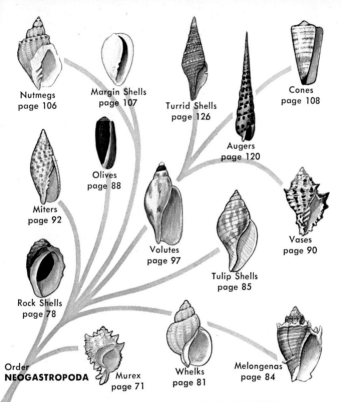

Nutmegs
page 106

Margin Shells
page 107

Turrid Shells
page 126

Cones
page 108

Olives
page 88

Augers
page 120

Miters
page 92

Volutes
page 97

Vases
page 90

Tulip Shells
page 85

Rock Shells
page 78

Order
NEOGASTROPODA

Murex
page 71

Whelks
page 81

Melongenas
page 84

MAJOR GROUPS OF MARINE SNAILS

From the primitive Slit Shells and their Limpet allies to the highly evolved Bubble Shells and Cones, the marine snails show great diversity in shape and sculpture. Of the hundred or so families of gastropods, 34 are pictured in this family key (with page numbers). They include the vast majority of the better-known sea snails which are apt to be found in amateur collections.

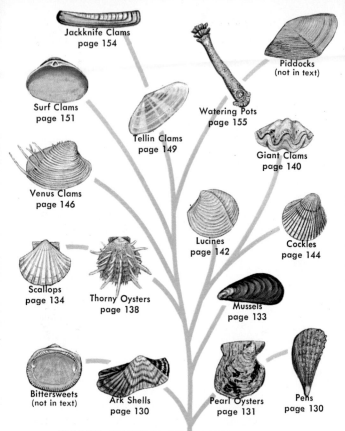

Jackknife Clams
page 154

Piddocks
(not in text)

Surf Clams
page 151

Watering Pots
page 155

Tellin Clams
page 149

Giant Clams
page 140

Venus Clams
page 146

Lucines
page 142

Cockles
page 144

Scallops
page 134

Thorny Oysters
page 138

Mussels
page 133

Bittersweets
(not in text)

Ark Shells
page 130

Pearl Oysters
page 131

Pens
page 130

MAJOR GROUPS OF MARINE BIVALVES

BIVALVES are less numerous than marine gastropods but are of greater economic value. Clams, oysters, mussels and scallops are eaten. One group produces nearly all natural and cultured pearls. The families shown on the tree are most commonly seen in collections.

OTHER GROUPS OF SEASHELLS

CEPHALOPODS include the octopus which has no shell and the squids with a thin internal shell. The Nautilus of the Indo-Pacific has a smooth, chambered shell. The Argonaut's paper-thin shell is an eggcase. Pages 156-157.

Chambered Nautilus 6"
Southwest Pacific
Nautilus pompilius L.

CHITONS are a group of flattened mollusks, some worm-like, most covered with eight shingle-like, overlapping plates held in place by a muscular ring called the girdle. They live on rocks near shore and feed on algae.

West Indian Chiton 2-3"
West Indies
Chiton tuberculata Linne

Hairy Mopalia 2"
Alaska to California
Mopalia ciliata Sby.

TUSK SHELLS, or Scaphopods, are tooth-shaped shells found in shallow and deep water. These odd mollusks are without gills (the mantle assumes this function), head, eyes or true tentacles. Some species were once highly valued by American Indians.

Money Tusk 1-2"
Alaska to California
Dentalium pretiosum Sby.

Elephant's Tusk 3"
Philippines
*Dentalium
elephantinum* L.

YOUR SHELL COLLECTION

A well-arranged, orderly collection of shells has many surprising rewards: a sense of scientific accomplishment, pride in building an educational and beautiful assortment, a stimulus to investigate an intriguing group of animals. Record locality data and best possible identification; follow a natural biological sequence, and your collection will serve as a useful guide and a constant source of satisfaction. Begin early to use a simple cabinet, multiple-sized paper trays, plastic boxes or match boxes, good labels, and a catalog with numbers corresponding to those written in India ink on the labels and specimens. Small shells, with numbered slips, may be put into glass vials, and the vials plugged with cotton.

A wooden cabinet (4 ft. high, 3 ft. deep and 2½ ft. wide) with wooden drawers on simple runners protects your shells from dust and careless hands.

JEANNE SCHWENGEL COLLECTION
NO. 22023
Volutoconus bednalli Brazier
Dredged in 30 ft., sand bottom.
40 miles N.E. of Darwin,
A.R. Cahn, coll. 1962   AUSTRALIA

Boxes made of cardboard of uniform height and of multiple sizes permit an orderly arrangement and best use of space.

Labels should bear the genus and species name. Most important are the locality data and other pertinent information.

COLLECTING MARINE SHELLS

BEACHCOMBING
Few mollusks live on the beach, but after storms fresh specimens may be cast ashore. Some appear only at certain seasons. Avoid damaged and water-worn shells.

NIGHT COLLECTING
Mollusks avoid bright sunlight. At low tide turn over rocks; dig in sand. Shore collecting at night in quiet bays is very profitable. Two people working together are most effective.

DIVING
Going down where many shells live brings rich rewards in perfect specimens. Watch for trails in the sand. Put shells in a fine mesh bag. Follow safety rules.

DREDGING
A simple wire-mesh dredge, 24" wide, 36" long and 8" high, can be pulled by rope at depths down to 100 feet. Wash sand away and pick out shells.

EXCHANGING
Trade with collectors in foreign lands. Send perfect specimens with locality data. Wrap securely. A good way to increase your collection and to make friends. Be as generous as possible.

BUYING SHELLS
Many reliable dealers sell specimen shells. Compare prices from several mail listings and then use good judgment. Insist on locality data. Avoid acid-treated shells.

PREPARING SHELLS FOR STUDY

When collecting, observe the live animals and note their habits. So little is known about many species that every accurate observation is of value. Note color and other details, relative abundance, type of bottom, food, egg-laying or mating habits, methods of concealment, water temperature, associated plants and animals. Record your facts in a field notebook. When cataloging, enter the notebook page on the collection label.

Make notes in the field. Keep accurate data. Clean and keep the specimens in your collection for future reference.

Observe the living mollusk in a glass jar or salt-water aquarium. Living animals may be photographed in color.

The soft parts and shells of mollusks may be permanently preserved in 70% alcohol. If not to be used for anatomical study, clams and snails may be boiled in water for five minutes and the "meat" removed with a bent pin or ice pick. Save the operculum, or trapdoor, to each snail. It is unwise to use acid on shells. Clean exterior with fine wire brush or buffing wheel.

MORE INFORMATION

Basic information about malacology, the study of mollusks, is found in thousands of monographs. Of greater use to collectors are the books listed below. Membership in local shell clubs will aid every collector. Write Secretary, Amer. Malacological Union, Box 318, Marinette, Wis., for information. Study the famous collections in natural history museums in Philadelphia, Washington, New York, Chicago, Los Angeles and San Francisco. Curators of these collections can give professional advice.

GENERAL BOOKS

Abbott, R. Tucker, SEASHELLS OF NORTH AMERICA, Golden Press, 1969. A guide to field identification of 900 species. Includes biology and collecting methods.

Johnstone, Kathleen Y., SEA TREASURE—A GUIDE TO SHELL COLLECTING, Houghton Mifflin Co., Boston, 1956. For beginners.

Morton, J. E., MOLLUSCS, Hutchinson & Co., London, 1958. Harper Torchbook Ed., 1960. An adult college-level treatment.

Wagner, R. J. L. and R. T. Abbott, VAN NOSTRAND'S STANDARD CATALOG OF SHELLS, D. Van Nostrand Co., Princeton, N. J., 1967. Lists thousands of species with current values.

NORTH AMERICA

Abbott, R. Tucker, AMERICAN SEASHELLS, D. Van Nostrand Co., Princeton, N. J., 1955. Mollusk biology, collecting methods, descriptions of 1500 species of both coasts; bibliography.

Keen, Myra, SEA SHELLS OF TROPICAL WEST AMERICA, Stanford Univ. Press, Calif., 1958. Excellent for tropical west Central America. Good bibliography.

Zim, H. S. & L. Ingle, SEASHORES, Golden Press, N. Y., 1955. Mollusks, other invertebrates, and marine plants. An elementary pocket guide with 213 common American mollusks.

FOREIGN

Allan, Joyce, AUSTRALIAN SHELLS, Georgian House, Melbourne, 1960.

Kira, T., JAPANESE SHELLS IN COLOR, Hoikusha Publ., Osaka, Japan, 1959. Many South Seas shells. Scientific names in English.

Powell, A. W. B., THE SHELLS OF NEW ZEALAND, Whitecombe and Tombs, London, 1946. The best for the area.

Warmke, G. and R. T. Abbott, CARIBBEAN SEASHELLS, Livingston Publ., Narberth, Pa., 1961. 840 West Indian marine mollusks.

THE WORLD OF MARINE SHELLS

Although the seas, which cover 72% of the earth's surface, are interconnected, parts of the oceans are isolated by land masses. Ocean currents, water temperatures and differences in salinity also act as barriers and create smaller sub-areas within faunistic provinces. Present faunistic boundaries were largely determined during the Pliocene, 10 million years ago. These are not clearly defined; some species invade the waters of neighboring provinces. Temperature is an important isolating factor. Within a province there may be special habitats suitable only to certain species—coral reefs, muddy or sandy bottoms, mangrove swamps or rocky shores. Some groups flourish in certain provinces, as the Limpets in South Africa and the Cowries in the Indo-Pacific. Some mollusks are associated only with certain other animals, such as the Wentletraps with sea anemones, and Rapa snails with soft corals.

COLD-WATER FAUNA
Few species; usually dull in color.

Astarte Clam

Colus Whelk

WARM-WATER FAUNA
Many species; usually bright in color.

Chama

Harpa

Cowrie

DISTRIBUTION OF MOLLUSKS WITH DEPTH

THE PELAGIC WORLD

Adults of about 100 species of mollusks live near the surface of the ocean. Some float, some are attached to sargassum weed, others hover in mid-water.

THE LITTORAL WORLD

A million miles of the world's intertidal shoreline support a rich fauna of Periwinkles, Limpets, burrowing clams, *Mytilus* and other species living between high- and low-tide level.

THE SHALLOW-WATER WORLD

Most of the marine mollusks live on the continental shelves and in coral reefs from the low-tide line to depths of about 400 feet. The relatively quiet waters and growth of algae permit a rich fauna to exist.

THE ABYSSAL WORLD

Small, mainly colorless shells live in the lightless depths of the ocean where temperatures are near freezing. Abyssal species are somewhat similar in all parts of the world. Squids have phosphorescent lights of blue, red and white.

Deep-sea mollusks living near the equator are found in much shallower waters in the polar seas where the water is cold. Some food comes from pelagic plants and animals which die and sink to the bottom. Both clams and snails have been found 3 miles down.

CALIFORNIAN PROVINCE

Stretching from Washington to parts of lower California is a cool-water fauna of about 2,100 species. To the north is the cold-water Aleutian Province, some of whose species find their way as far south as northern California. In southern California, elements of the Panamic Province, a much warmer area, begin to apear. The Californian Province is rich in Abalones, Murex Rock Shells, Limpets and Chitons. Among some of the characteristic species are the Kelp-weed Scallop and the Purple Dwarf Olive.

Frilled Dogwinkle
Nucella lamellosa Gmel.

Purple Dwarf Olive
Olivella biplicata Sby.

Chitons
Over 50 species

Kelp-weed Scallop
Leptopecten latiauratus Con.

Haliotis **Abalones**
Several large species

Cooper's Nutmeg
Cancellaria cooperi Con.

CAROLINIAN PROVINCE

From the south shore of Cape Cod, Mass., to the northern half of Florida and westward into Texas, the temperate-water Carolinian Province is characterized by Quahog Clams, *Mercenaria*, and by such species as the Shark-eye Moon Snail and the Marsh Periwinkle. The southern tip of Florida belongs to the tropical Caribbean Province. To the north, from Maine to Labrador, is the colder Boreal Province with a different and less rich shell fauna. The New England Neptune lives to the north.

Marsh Periwinkle
Littorina irrorata Say

Shark-eye Moon Snail
Polinices duplicatus Say

Quahog Clam
Mercenaria mercenaria L.

New England Neptune
Neptunea decemcostata Say
New England and north

Oyster Drill
Eupleura caudata Say

CHINA

INDIA

AFRICA

Lambis

Tibia

AUSTRALIA

INDO-PACIFIC PROVINCE

The largest and richest shell region in the world extends from the shores of East Africa eastward through the East Indies to Polynesia. Notable for its abundance of colorful shells, it supports many strange and unique mollusks, such as the Giant Clams *(Tridacna)*, the Scorpion Conchs *(Lambis)*, and the Heart Cockles *(Corculum)*. Most of the Indo-Pacific is characterized by tropical waters and coral reefs. The province is further divided into more or less isolated sub-regions.

Lineated Conch
Strombus fasciatus Born

THE RED SEA is an isolated, warm-water pocket of the Indian Ocean noted for its many peculiar subspecies and such unique species as the Lineated Conch *(Strombus fasciatus* Born), and Red-spotted Cowrie *(Cypraea erythraeenis* Sby.).

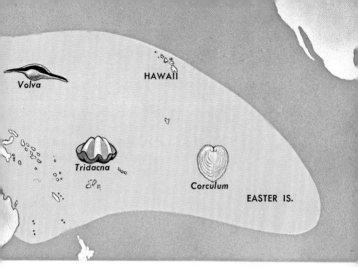

Volva

HAWAII

Tridacna

Corculum

EASTER IS.

AUSTRALIA is, along its tropical northern half, a land of rare and colorful Volutes and strange Spiny Vase Shells *(Tudicula)*. The seas are shallow with strong tides. The seas of southern Australia are much colder and have many different shells, such as the Giant Phasianellas.

Bednall's Volute
Volutoconus bednalli Braz.

THE HAWAIIAN CHAIN of volcanic islands in the central Pacific lacks many common Indo-Pacific species. It has some unique cowries and cone shells. The Tiger Cowrie, common elsewhere, is rare here and very large.

Tessellate Cowrie
Cypraea tessellata Sw.

THE PHILIPPINES, consisting of thousands of islands, are very rich in mollusks. Several unique kinds are found in these waters, including the Imperial Volute and the rare Glory-of-the-Seas Cone. Some normally uncommon species are abundant on the reefs of Philippine islands.

Imperial Volute
Aulica imperialis Ltft.

PANAMIC PROVINCE

From the Gulf of California to northern Ecuador, the tropical Panamic Province supports a rich, colorful fauna of over 2,000 marine shells. Connected with the Caribbean in former geologic times, the fauna resembles that of the West Indies. Tidal ranges are extreme in this area. The genus *Strombina,* and such species as the Tent Olive are native.

Tent Olive
Oliva porphyria L.

Radix Murex
Murex radix Gmel.

Grinning Tun
Malea ringens Sw.

***Strombina* Whelks**
Several species

SOUTH AMERICA

CARIBBEAN PROVINCE

Centered in the West Indies, this tropical province extends north to the Florida Keys and Bermuda. Many Caribbean elements spread out to the south as far as Brazil. Among the characteristic species are the Queen Conch, the Wide-mouthed Purpura and the Sunrise Tellin. The fauna is rich in *Cassis*, *Murex* and *Tellina*. The larger West Indian islands have over 1,200 species of shelled marine mollusks. Isolated coral islands, poor in food, have only about 350 kinds of mollusks.

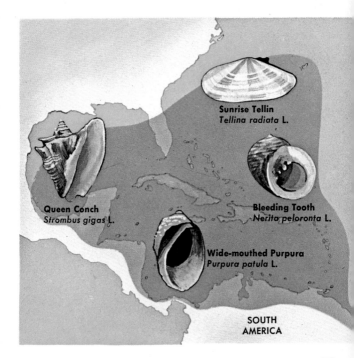

Sunrise Tellin
Tellina radiata L.

Queen Conch
Strombus gigas L.

Bleeding Tooth
Nerita peloronta L.

Wide-mouthed Purpura
Purpura patula L.

SOUTH
AMERICA

MEDITERRANEAN PROVINCE

The most isolated of the world's major seas, the Mediterranean, is relatively shallow and less dense than the Atlantic. Its fauna of 1,400 species of mollusks spreads around Portugal to southern France and along the northwest coast of Africa. Also known as the Lusitanian Province, it contains such unique shells as the Pelican's Foot, Jacob's Scallop, and the Murex Dye Shells.

Lurid Cowrie
Cypraea lurida L.

Spiny Helmet
Galeodea echinophora L.

Jacob's Scallop
Pecten jacobaeus L.

Purple Dye Murex
Murex brandaris L.

Pelican's Foot
Aporrhais pes-pelicani L.

JAPANESE PROVINCE

Lying between the cold-water Aleutian Province and the tropical Indo-Pacific, the central islands of Japan contain a rich and distinct temperate marine fauna.

Miraculous Thatcheria
Thatcheria mirabilis
Sby.

JAPAN

Japanese Babylon
Babylonia japonica
Rve.

Slit Shells
Pleurotomaria

SOUTH AFRICAN PROVINCE

Cool, rough seas pound the rocky shoreline of South Africa. Its isolated fauna of about 900 species is rich in giant Limpets, Turbans and Thais Rock Shells, plus strange, cool-water cowries and cone shells.

AFRICA

Patella Limpets
21 species

Rosy Cone
Conus aurora Lam.

Cape Cowrie
Cypraea capensis Gray

heart · stomach · gills · mantle · brain · tentacle · eye · proboscis · digestive gland · gonads · rectum · operculum · foot

cross section of proboscis

radular ribbon · mouth

egg capsule · eggs

radular teeth enlarged

free-swimming veliger

GASTROPODS, or Univalves, single-shelled mollusks, include Snails, Conchs, Periwinkles and Whelks. About half of the 80,000 species are marine; the remainder are terrestrial and fresh-water. The fleshy, cape-like mantle produces a hard shell, while the foot may produce a horny operculum. Feeding is aided by a special set of teeth known as the radula. The sexes are separate in many marine species. Eggs are laid into the water or in capsules. A free-swimming larva, or "veliger," emerges which grows into a shelled adult. Most gastropods live 5-6 years; some may survive 20 or 30. Univalves may be carnivorous, herbivorous or even parasitic.

SLIT SHELLS (Pleurotomariidae) are primitive snails characterized by two gill plumes. The slit in the shell is a natural opening for the passage of water and waste materials. The family, found in very early fossil deposits, was once considered to be extinct. Today 8 living deep-water species are known.

The operculum of the Slit Shells is thin, corneous, and brown and has many whorls.

This relatively small operculum is attached to the foot.

Emperor's Slit Shell 3-5"
Pleurotomaria hirasei Pilsbry
Honshu Is., Japan
This is the commonest Slit Shell known. It lives at a depth of 300 feet.

Adanson's Slit Shell 5-6"
P. adansonianus Cr. & Fisch.
W. Indies; deep water; rare

Beyrich's Slit Shell 4"
P. beyrichi Hilgen.
E. Asia; deep water; rare

anal slit

ABALONE shells (Haliotidae) resemble a valve of a large clam, except for the spiral whorl. The animal has a large, flat and muscular foot by which it holds fast to rocks. Sea water is drawn in under the edges of the shell; it passes over the gills, and leaves through the natural holes. The foot is edible and highly esteemed. The iridescent shell is used in costume jewelry. Over a hundred species are known. They are vegetarians.

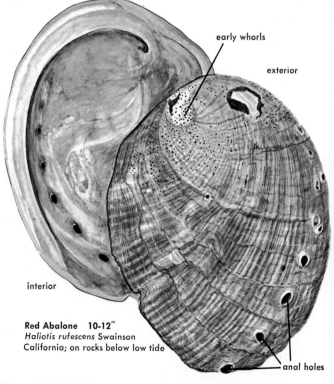

early whorls

exterior

interior

Red Abalone 10-12″
Haliotis rufescens Swainson
California; on rocks below low tide

anal holes

Black Abalone 5″
Haliotis cracherodi Leach
California to Mexico

Pink Abalone 5-7″
Haliotis corrugata Gray
California

Beautiful Abalone 1-1½″
H. pulcherrima Gmelin
Central Pacific

Donkey's Ear Abalone 3-4″
Haliotis asinina Linné
S.W. Pacific

Midas Abalone 4″
Haliotis midae Linné
South Africa

KEYHOLE LIMPETS (Fissurellidae) are named for a small hole at the top of the cap-shaped shell, which serves for excretion. Several hundred species are all vegetarians living in shallow, warm water. The single eggs are coated with a gelatinous sheath. The largest comes from California.

Maximum Keyhole Limpet   3"
Fissurella maxima Sowerby
Chile (intertidal)

Giant Keyhole Limpet   4-5"
Megathura crenulata Sby.
Calif. (intertidal)

Barbados Keyhole Limpet   1"
Fissurella barbadensis Gmel.
Florida and W. Indies

Roman Shield Limpet *(Scutus)* from Australia has no hole but is related to the Keyhole Limpets. The shell is 2 inches long.

side view of living animal

shell

TRUE LIMPETS (Acmaeidae) live on the rocky shores of all temperate seas. They have a remarkably strong foot. A few species attach to seaweeds. All 400 species are vegetarian.

Sweet Limpet 1″
A. saccharina Linné
Indo-Pacific; common

Atlantic Plate Limpet 1″
Acmaea testudinalis Müller
New England rocks; common

Unstable Limpet 1″
A. instabilis Gould
California; on seaweed

Spiked Limpet 3″
Patella longicosta Lam.
South Africa

TOP SHELLS (Trochidae) are conical. They have a pearly interior and a thin, horny operculum with many whorls. Over a thousand species are found mainly in temperate and tropical waters. Largest and most useful is the Commercial Trochus, from which shirt buttons are made. Some larger species are eaten. A trochus takes six years to reach adult size—5 inches. All Top Shells are vegetarians.

Knobbed Top   4"   ▶
Trochus dentatus Forsk.
East Africa; common

Giant Button Top   1"
Umbonium giganteum Less.
Japan; muddy bays; abundant

underside

Lined Top   2"
Trochus lineatus Lam.
Australia; common in shallow water

Strawberry Top   1"
Clanculus puniceus Phil.
Indian Ocean; common

INDO-PACIFIC TOP SHELLS vary greatly in form and color. The Button Tops *(Umbonium)*, mud-dwellers from Japan and Southeast Asia, are unusually flattened.

young

Pyramid Top 5″ ▶
Tectus pyramis Born

Maculated Top 2″
Trochus maculatus L.
A very common species
found under rocks near shore.

Born's Orange Top ¾″ ▶
Chlorostoma paradoxum
Born

◀ **Commercial Trochus 5″**
Trochus niloticus L.

operculum

AMERICAN TOP SHELLS total several dozen species, rarest being the iridescent Gaza. The West Indian Top is used in chowder. Queen Tegula is a collector's item in California. Norris' Top Shell is relatively common in shallow water. Its operculum bears tiny bristles.

Queen Tegula 2″
Tegula regina Stearns
So. California; deep water

Superb Gaza 2″
Gaza superba Dall
Gulf of Mexico; deep water

Norris' Top Shell 2″
Norrisia norrisi Sby.
California; near shore

West Indian Top 3″
Cittarium pica L.
W. Indies; seashore

operculum
of *Cittarium*

CALLIOSTOMA TOP SHELLS are the queens of the family. All are light-weight shells with delicate beading and bright colors. Most are cold-water inhabitants found among deep-water beds of algae. Many are considered collector's items. Eggs are in gelatinous ribbons.

◄ **Cunningham's Top.** This is one of a dozen large, stunning species found in New Zealand. *Maurea cunninghami* G. and P. 3″

Monile Top 1″
Calliostoma monile Reeve
N.W. Australia; common
near shore on sponge

Haliarchus Top 2″
Calliostoma haliarchus Melvill
Japan; deep water

Chocolate-Lined Top 1″
Calliostoma javanicum Lam.
So. Fla. and Carib.

TURBAN SHELLS (Turbinidae), about 500 species, possess a hard, limy operculum. The largest member of the family is the Green Turban. Its white operculum may weigh up to one pound. Buttons are made from the shells.

Green Turban   8″ ▶
Turbo marmoratus L.
E. Indies-Australia

Chestnut Turban   1½″
Turbo castanea Gmel.
Florida-W. Indies

inner side

outer side   operculum

◀ **Tapestry Turban** is a herbivorous species of South Pacific coral reefs. The shell has a variable and colorful pattern. Its operculum is the famous blue-green "cat's eye." *(Turbo petholatus* L.) 3″.

PHEASANT AND STAR SHELLS are turbans. The Pheasant Shells have several "foot feelers." Below is the largest, the Pheasant Shell, *Phasianella australis* Gmel. (3 in.) from southern Australia. There are about 40 species.

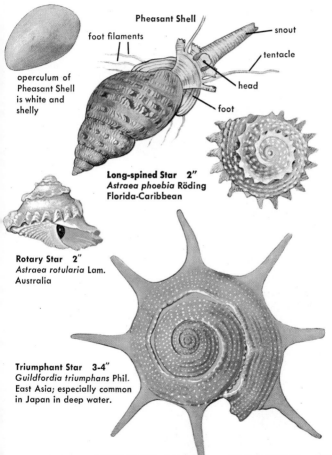

Pheasant Shell

foot filaments

snout

tentacle

head

foot

operculum of
Pheasant Shell
is white and
shelly

Long-spined Star   2"
Astraea phoebia Röding
Florida-Caribbean

Rotary Star   2"
Astraea rotularia Lam.
Australia

Triumphant Star   3-4"
Guildfordia triumphans Phil.
East Asia; especially common
in Japan in deep water.

COMMON INDO-PACIFIC TURBANS

Of the several dozen Turbans from the tropical Western Pacific, these are the commonest. Note the characteristic shape of the operculum in each species.

Horned Turban   3"
Turbo cornutus Lightfoot
Southern Japan; common near shore

Gold-mouthed Turban   3"
Turbo chrysostomus L.
Common on coral reefs

Dwarf Turban   1½"   **Silver-mouthed Turban   3"**   **Setose Turban   3"**
T. bruneus Röd.   *Turbo argyrostomus* L.   *T. setosus* Gm.

Sydney Turban 3½″ *Turbo torquatus* Gmelin. South Australia; common in shallow water; note the peculiar, white operculum.

South African Turban 3″ *Turbo sarmaticus* Linné. South Africa. This shell is pearly white and red when polished.

Two forms of the Delphinula Snail

Channelled Turban from the West Indies is rarest in the Americas. *Turbo canaliculatus* Herm. 3″.

Delphinula Snail from the Indo-Pacific reefs is very variable and has a brown, horny operculum. *Angaria delphinus* L. 2″ ▶

NERITE SNAILS (Neritidae) are of a family with varied habitats: shallow water, rocky shores, springs, rivers, swamps and even in trees. The Emerald Nerite lives on eelgrass near coral reefs. The shelly operculum bears a small projecting arm for muscular attachment. Nerites are vegetarians living in large colonies. Several hundred species are known.

Polita Nerite 1"
Nerita polita Linné
Indo-Pacific; common

operculum

inner side

outer side

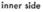

capsule with young

Living Nerite

egg capsules on rocks

Bleeding Tooth 2"
Nerita peloronta L.
S. Florida-Caribbean

Ornate Nerite 2"
Nerita ornata Sby.
Panama (Pacific)

Emerald Nerite ⅓"
Smaragdia viridis L.
Florida-Caribbean

PERIWINKLES (Littorinidae) are found on rocky shores of most parts of the world. Their small size and drab colors protect them from predators. The microscopic eggs laid in the water resemble miniature "flying saucers." Eggs of some species hatch inside oviduct.

side view of animal

Common European Periwinkle. Once limited to Europe and Canada, this rock-dweller has spread south to Delaware in the last 200 years. Shells have been found in prehistoric Indian sites. *Littorina littorea* L. 1"

Pagoda Periwinkle 2" ▶
Tectarius pagodus L.
Indo-Pacific; common on rocks well above high-tide line

◀ **Auger Turritella 4"**
Turritella terebra L.
Indo-Pacific

TURRITELLA SNAILS (Turritellidae), about 50 species, are tropical relatives of the Periwinkles. The shells, found in shallow, muddy bottoms, are long and pointed. The corneous operculum has few whorls.

SUNDIALS (Architectonicidae) resemble a winding staircase. All 40 species are tropical. A few deep-sea species are collector's items. Operculum like horny pill.

Common Atlantic Sundial   2″
Architectonica nobilis Röding
Carolinas to West Indies; common in sand

Variegated Sundial   ¾″
Heliacus variegatus Gmelin
Indo-Pacific

young
Worm Shell

Florida Worm Shell   4″ ▶
Vermicularia knorri Deshayes
Carolinas to Mexico

adult

WORMSHELLS resemble marine worms, but are true snails. The early whorls resemble Turritella Shells, but later ones detach and grow haphazardly.

CERITHS

Giant Knobbed Cerith 4"
Cerithium nodulosum Brug.
Indo-Pacific; abundant

Sowerby's Cerith 4"
C. sowerbyi Kiener
Philippines; uncommon

Common Vertegus 2"
Rhinoclavis vertagus L.
Indo-Pacific; abundant

Sulcate Cerith 2"
Terebralia sulcata Born
Indo-Pacific; swamps

Radula Cerith 2"
Tympanotonus radula L.
W. African swamps

CERITHS (Cerithiidae), about 300 species, are abundant in the intertidal zone of tropic shores. Some live in mangrove swamps, others at sea. The eggs are in jelly masses.

WENTLETRAPS (Epitoniidae), a curious family mainly alabaster-white, are capable of excreting a purple dye. Most are found with sea anemones and Fungia corals. Rice-paste counterfeits of the rare Precious Wentletrap were once sold. About 200 known species, some rare.

◄ **Common Wentletrap** 1"
Epitonium clathrus L.
Europe; common

▲
Noble Wentletrap 2"
Sthenorytis pernobilis
Fisch. & Bern.
Florida-Caribbean; rare

Precious Wentletrap 2"
Epitonium scalare Linné
Eastern Asia; uncommon

Magnificent Wentletrap 4"
Amaea magnifica Sby.
Japan; rare

CUP AND SLIPPER SHELLS possess a peculiar plate located inside the main shell. These limpet-like snails live in shallow water. The males are much smaller, but may change their sex and grow to a larger size. The Slipper Shells may grow on top of each other or on rocks.

Common Atlantic Slipper Shell   2″
Crepidula fornicata Linné
Canada to Texas; Europe; very common
This, like other Slipper Shells, has no operculum.

Imbricate Cup-and-Saucer   2″
Crucibulum scutellatum Wood
West Mexico

Rayed Peruvian Hat   2″
Trochita trochiformis Born
Peru and Chile

THE TRUE CONCHS

Eighty world species of Strombidae live in warm waters. Note the "notch" on the lower outer lip. The foot is narrow and muscular with a sharp, sickle-shaped operculum.

foot — eye — snout — operculum

Colorful eyes on special stalks are characteristic for each species. Above are four examples.

Queen Conch 8-12" *Strombus gigas* Linné. Southern Florida-West Indies. This large Caribbean Conch shell has long been a favorite ornament. Conch chowder and steak come from this species, and its shell is used as a trumpet. The young "rollers" do not have the flaring, thick lip of the 12-in. adults. Semi-precious pink pearls have been found inside the shells. The animal feeds on delicate algae. Females may be larger.

Florida Fighting Conch 2-3"
Strombus alatus Gmelin
Florida; common near shore
▼

West Indian Fighting Conch 2-3"
Strombus pugilis Linné
Caribbean; common near shore
▼

Goliath Conch   15″ ▶
Strombus goliath Schröter
Brazil; rare

Rooster Conch   5″
Strombus gallus
Linné
Caribbean ▼

Two of these Atlantic Conchs are collector's items. Rarest is the Goliath Conch from Brazil, largest *Strombus* in the world. The Rooster Conch of the Caribbean region is fairly rare. Adults vary in size; the male is smaller. In the Milk Conch, the size and number of knobs is variable, and some shells may be orange, yellow, or whitish. 1½″ dwarfs of the Hawk-Wing occur in Lake Worth, Florida.

Milk Conch   4-7″
S. costatus Gmelin
Caribbean ▼

Hawk-Wing Conch 2-4″ ▶
S. raninus Gmelin
Caribbean

COMMON INDIO-PACIFIC CONCHS—1-3 IN. LONG

Bubble Conch
Strombus bulla Röding

Diana Conch
S. aurisdianae L.

Dog Conch
S. canarium L.

Humped Conch
S. gibberulus L.

Mutable Conch
S. mutabilis Swain.

Little Bear Conch
Strombus urceus L.

black mouth

white mouth

◄ **Silver Conch**
S. lentiginosus Linné

Blood-Mouth Conch
S. luhuanus Linné

UNUSUAL CONCHS

Bull Conch is a rare species from the coral reefs in the Central Pacific. Shell heavy with two unique spines on outer lip. 4". *Strombus taurus* Rve. Found at depths of 20 to 50 feet.

Laciniated Conch is an uncommon and attractive W. Pacific shell noted for the beautiful purple interior of its mouth. 4". *Strombus sinuatus* Lightfoot

Little Frog Conch 4"
Strombus latus Gmelin
West African and Cape Verde Is.

Peruvian Conch 6" ►
Strombus peruvianus Sw.
Pacific side of
Central America

SPIDER CONCHS (Strombidae) are closely related to the true Conchs. The ten known species of Spider Conchs are limited to the tropical waters of the Indo-Pacific region. A fossil species is found in Hawaii. All are vegetarians and lay spaghetti-like egg masses.

Arthritic Spider Conch   6"
◀ *L. arthritica* Röding
Indian Ocean; uncommon

Chiragra Spider Conch   7" ▶
Lambis chiragra L.
S.W. Pacific; common

▲
Violet Spider Conch   3-4"
L. violacea Swain.
Mauritius; rare

Scorpion Conch 4-5"
L. scorpius L. ▶
Uncommon

◀ **Common Spider Conch** 4"
Lambis lambis L.
Indo-Pacific; abundant

Orange Spider Conch
3-4" ▶
L. crocata Link
Uncommon

Giant Spider Conch 12"
Lambis truncata Lightfoot
Indian Ocean; common
▼

◀ **Milleped Spider Conch** 5"
L. millepeda L.
S.W. Pacific; common

SPIDER CONCHS **47**

CARRIER AND TIBIA SHELLS

1.

CARRIER SHELLS include the Japanese Carrier Shell (1) *Xenophora pallidula* Reeve, 4 in., which attaches dead shells to itself. (2) The Sunburst Carrier, *Stellaria solaris* Linné, 3 in., from the Western Pacific, develops its own limy projections. The animals are very active.

TIBIA SHELLS, long and slender, are from the Philippines. (3) Spindle Tibia, *Tibia fusus* L., reaches 12 in. (4) Dwarf Tibia, *Varicospira cancellata* L., is 1 in. All are collector's items.

3.

2.

4.

MOON SNAILS

tentacle

shell

Shell of Moon Snail is en-
veloped by large gray foot.

propodium

MOON SNAILS are found on sandy flats in nearly all parts of the world. They spend most of their time digging through the sand in search of clams and smaller snails. They drill a neat hole through the shell of their prey and rasp out the meat. Their foot is large and covers much of the shell when it is extended. Egg-masses are laid in collar-shaped cases made with fine sand. These are often found at low tide. The young hatch out in 2 or 3 weeks.

Operculum, or trapdoor, which seals the mouth of *Polinices* and Lunatia Moon Snails is thin and horny. Some are brown; others are red.

Albumen Moon Snail   2″ ▶
Polinices albumen L. Indo-Pacific

Northern Moon Snail   4″
Lunatia heros Say
Canada to Virginia

Atlantic Shark Eye   2″
P. duplicatus Say
Mass. to Texas

Operculum of Moon Snails in the genus *Natica* is hard and shell-like. Most members of this genus (over 100 species) live in sandy tropical bays; some live in the Arctic. A. Attachment side. B. Outer side.

China Moon 1"
Natica onca Röding
Indo-Pacific; a moderately common species found in sand below low tide.

Zebra Moon 1"
N. zebra Lamarck
Indo-Pacific

Butterfly Moon 1½"
N. alapapilionis Röd.
Indo-Pacific; also found in sand but uncommon

Maculated Moon 1"
N. tigrina Röding
Indo-Pacific ▼

Stellate Moon 2-3"
N. stellata Chenu, 1845
Japan ▼

Colorful Atlantic Moon
N. canrena Linné
Florida-Caribbean 1-2"

COWRIES

shell

siphon
tentacle
snout

mantle

foot

Tiger Cowrie with its fleshy mantle partly covering its shell.

When disturbed, its mantle con-
tracts, revealing the glossy shell.

COWRIES, with glossy, china-like shells, attracted primitive peoples who used them as ornaments, money and as
religious symbols. Today, cowries rank high with shell
collectors. Most of the 160 or so species are relatively
common in tropical seas. A few are very rare. The hard
shell and attractive colors are produced by the envelop-
ing fleshy mantle. Cowries are active at night, feeding on
hydroids and similar small marine creatures.

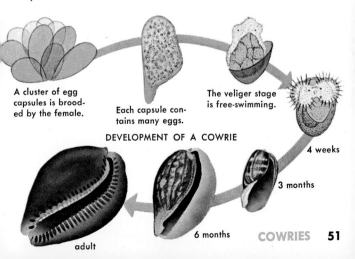

A cluster of egg
capsules is brood-
ed by the female.

Each capsule con-
tains many eggs.

The veliger stage
is free-swimming.

DEVELOPMENT OF A COWRIE

4 weeks

3 months

6 months

adult

COWRIES   51

Atlantic Gray Cowrie 1"
Cypraea cinerea
Gmel.
Florida-Caribbean

Atlantic Yellow Cowrie 1"
C. spurca acicularis Gmel.
Florida-Caribbean

AMERICAN COWRIES

American tropical waters have less than a dozen species of cowries. Four Atlantic species are found in Florida, and the uncommon Mouse Cowrie is limited to the lower Caribbean.

Measled Cowrie 3"
Cypraea zebra Linné
Florida-Caribbean

Chestnut Cowrie 2"
Cypraea spadicea Swain.
Southern California

Mouse Cowrie 2"
Cypraea mus L.
Venezuela

Panama Cowrie 2"
Cypraea cervinetta Kien.
Gulf of Panama

Atlantic Deer Cowrie 4"
Cypraea cervus L.
Florida-Cuba-Yucatan

AFRICAN COWRIES

South African waters are the home of seven cowries; six of them are relatively common. Fulton's Cowrie is one of the world's rarest, found in the stomachs of the Mussel Cracker fish which feeds on it.

Brown-Toothed Cowrie   1½″
Cypraea angustata Gmel.

Cape Cowrie   1″
Cypraea capensis Gray

Toothless Cowrie   1″
Cypraea edentula Gray

Fulton's Cowrie   2″
Cypraea fultoni Sowerby
▼

Rat Cowrie   3″
Cypraea stercoraria L.
West Africa

PANAMIC (PACIFIC) COWRIES

Little Arabian Cowrie ¾"
Cypraea arabicula Lam.

Black-spotted Cowrie 1-1½"
C. nigropunctata Gray
Galapagos Is.

Roberts' Cowrie 1"
C. robertsi Hidalgo

MEDITERRANEAN COWRIES

Agate Cowrie 1"
C. achatidea Sby.

Pear Cowrie 1"
C. pyrum Gmel.

Lurid Cowrie 1½"
C. lurida L.

Zoned Cowrie 1½"
C. zonaria Gmel.
West Africa

Spurca Cowrie ¾"
C. spurca L.

AUSTRALIAN COWRIES

Thersite Cowrie 3"
C. thersites Gask.

Friend's Cowrie 3"
Cypraea friendii Gray

Armenian Cowrie 4"
Cypraea armeniaca Verco
Western Australia; deep
water; rare

under view

side view

Umbilicate Cowrie 4"
C. hesitata Iredale
Deep water; New South Wales
▼

Decipiens Cowrie 2"
Cypraea decipiens E. A. Smith
▼

Albino form of the ▶
Umbilicate Cowrie 4"
C. hesitata form *alba* Cox

COMMON INDO-PACIFIC COWRIES (2" or less)

Pacific Deer Cowrie 2"
C. *vitellus* Linné

Coloba Cowrie 1"
C. *coloba* Melvill
Indian Ocean

Chinese Cowrie 1½"
C. *chinensis* Gmelin

Tahitian Gold-ringer ½"
C. *obvelata* Lamarck
Society Islands

Caurica Cowrie 1½"
C. *caurica* Linné

Gold-ringer ½-1"
C. *annulus* Linné
Very common

Lynx Cowrie 1-2"
C. *lynx* Linné

Camel Cowrie 2"
C. *camelopardalis* Perry
Red Sea; uncommon

COMMON INDO-PACIFIC COWRIES (2-4")

Tiger Cowrie
Cypraea tigris Linné

Panther Cowrie (Red Sea)
C. pantherina Lightfoot

Arabian Cowrie
C. arabica Linné

Histrio Cowrie
C. histrio Gmelin

Eglantine Cowrie
C. eglantina Duclos

Reticulated Cowrie
C. maculifera Schilder

Eyed Cowrie
Cypraea argus Linné
Uncommon

Mole Cowrie
Cypraea talpa Linné

COMMON INDO-PACIFIC COWRIES

Ventriculate Cowrie   2"
C. ventriculus Lam.

Carnelian Cowrie   2"
C. carneola L.

Ocellate Cowrie   1"
C. ocellata L.
Indian Ocean only

Isabelle Cowrie   1"
C. isabella L.

Tortoise Cowrie   4"
C. testudinaria L.

**Grooved-toothed
Cowrie   1½"**
C. sulcidentata Gray
Hawaii

Schilder's Cowrie   1½"
C. schilderorum Ire.

Hump-back Cowrie   3"
C. mauritiana L.
Commonest on this page.

COMMON INDO-PACIFIC COWRIES (1-2")

Snake-head Cowrie
C. caputserpentis L.
Very common

Lamarck's Cowrie
C. lamarcki Gray

Dragon-head Cowrie
C. caputdraconis Melv.
Easter Island; uncommon

Thrush Cowrie
C. turdus Lam.
Indian Ocean

Boivin's Cowrie
C. boivini Kiener

Miliaris Cowrie
C. miliaris Gmel.

Eroded Cowrie
Cypraea erosa L.

Onyx Cowrie
Cypraea onyx L.

Wandering Cowrie
Cypraea errones L.

UNCOMMON INDO-PACIFIC COWRIES

The cowries on these two pages occur in various parts of the Indo-Pacific. Most are uncommon. Most sought after are the Map, Cox's and Stolid Cowries.

Dawn Cowrie ¾"
C. *diluculum* Rve.
East Africa

Porous Cowrie ¾"
C. *poraria* L.
South Pacific

Tapering Cowrie 1"
Cypraea *teres* L.

Cox's Cowrie ¾"
C. *coxeni* Cox

◀ **Cylindrical Cowrie** 1"
C. *cylindrica* Born

Walker's Cowrie 1"
C. *walkeri* Sby. ▶

◀ **Sieve Cowrie** 1"
C. *cribraria* L.

Zig-Zag Cowrie ½"
C. *ziczac* L. ▶
Uncommon

Honey Cowrie 1″
C. *helvola* L.

Map Cowrie 4″
C. *mappa* L.
A popular collector's item.
▼

Stolid Cowrie 1″
C. *stolida* L.
Moderately common

Punctate Cowrie
C. *punctata* L. ⅓″

Asellus Cowrie ½″
C. *asellus* L.

◄ **Jester Cowrie** 1-1½″
C. *scurra* Gmel.
Uncommon; two views ►

◄ **Nucleus Cowrie** ¾″
C. *nucleus* Linné

Chick-Pea Cowrie ½″
C. *cicercula* Linné ►

◄ **Money Cowrie** 1″
C. *moneta* Linné
Very common

Kitten Cowrie ½″
C. *felina* Gmelin ►

SOME RARE COWRIES

Seldom seen in amateur collections, but greatly sought after, are several rare cowries, some worth several hundreds of dollars.

◄ The **Golden Cowrie** is not exceedingly rare, but is a choice collector's item from Melanesia. 4″ *Cypraea aurantium* Gmel.

Rare Spotted Cowrie   2″
Cypraea guttata Gmel.
Central Pacific; very rare

Leucodon Cowrie   3″
Cypraea leucodon Brod.
Philippines; very rare

Broderip's Cowrie   3″
Cypraea broderipii Sby.
Indian Ocean; very rare

THE HELMET SHELLS

The large, massive Helmet Shells (Cassidae) are found in tropical waters around the world. They live in shallow water on sandy bottoms and feed mainly on sea urchins. The larger ones are used in making shell cameos.

King Helmet   7"
Cassis tuberosa L.
Caribbean

Tessellate Helmet   6-9"
Cassis tessellata Gmel.
West Africa
Uncommon

Horned Helmet   10"
Cassis cornuta L.
Indo-Pacific

Scotch Bonnet 3"
Phalium granulatum Born
S.E. U.S.-Caribbean

Smooth Scotch Bonnet 3"
Phalium granulatum
form *cicatricosum* Gmelin
Fla.-Caribbean

Gray Bonnet 4"
Phalium glaucum Linné
Indo-Pacific; uncommon

Striped Bonnet 3"
Phalium strigatum Gmelin
Indo-Pacific

note channel

Channelled Bonnet 2"
P. canaliculata Brug.
Indo-Pacific

Areola Bonnet 2"
Phalium areola L.
Indo-Pacific

Japanese Bonnet 3"
P. bisulcatum Sch.
and Wag.
Japan

Vibex Bonnet of the Indo-Pacific is very variable in shape, some specimens being smooth (right fig.), others with knobs on the shoulder (left fig.). 1-2". *Casmaria erinaceus* Linné

Iredale's Bonnet 3" ▶
Phalium iredalei Baye
South Africa

Adult Red Helmets have no operculum. The animal is orange-red. Cameos are made from the large Bull Mouth Helmet of the Indian Ocean which lives in shallow water.

Bull Mouth Helmet 6"
Cypraecassis rufa L.; Indian Ocean
▼

Contracted Cowrie-helmet 3"
C. coarctata Sowerby; Panama

Reticulated Cowrie-helmet 3"
C. testiculus L.; Caribbean

HELMET SHELLS

Prickly Helmet   3″
Galeodea echinophora L.
Mediterranean

Tuscan Helmet   3″
G. *rugosa* L.
Mediterranean

Atlantic Woodlouse   1″
Morum oniscus L.
Caribbean; common

Cancellate Morum   1½″
Morum cancellatum Sby.
Southeast Asia

Royal Bonnet   2″
Sconsia striata Lam.
Caribbean; deep water

Exquisite Morum   1½″
Morum exquisitum Ads. & Rve.
Philippines; rare

THE FROG SHELLS

The tropical Frog Shells (Bursidae) are represented by several genera and about 60 species, ranging in size from ½" to 10". Large ones were once used for oil lamps.

Gyrate Frogshell   1"
Gyrineum gyrinum L.
Indo-Pacific

Winged Frog Shell   3"
Biplex perca Perry
Southeast Asia

Granulated Frog Shell   2"
Bursa granularis Röd.
Caribbean and Indo-Pacific
A common snail found on
reefs under rocks.

Giant Frog Shell   5-10" ▶
Bursa bubo L.; Indo-Pacific
Moderately common near
coral reefs.

Spiny Frog Shell   2-3"
Bursa spinosa Lam.
Indo-Pacific ▼

THE TRITON TRUMPETS

There are less than a dozen species of these large Triton Trumpets. Most occur in tropical waters near coral reefs. By cutting off the end of the spire or making a round hole in the side, natives use the large species as trumpets. All members of the family Cymatiidae have horny opercula.

The Caribbean and the Indo-Pacific Triton Trumpets are very closely related. The former has thin, raised teeth on the inner lip; the latter has wider, flattened teeth, as shown below.

Pacific Triton   8-15"
Charonia tritonis L.

Atlantic Triton   8-11"
Charonia variegata Lam.

Pustuled Triton   5" ▶
Charonia pustulata Lam.
South Africa

Knobbed Triton   10-16"
Charonia nodifera Lam.
Mediterranean

THE HAIRY TRITONS

Most of the hundred species of Hairy Tritons (family Cymatiidae) are characterized by a periostracum of "hairs" covering the outside of the shell. The family is mainly tropical. Hairy Tritons are carnivorous. They lay numerous horny egg capsules on rocks.

Common Hairy Triton   3-4"
Cymatium pileare L.
Caribbean and Indo-Pacific
Common on coral reefs.

Lotorium Triton   5"
Cymatium lotorium L.
Indo-Pacific; moderately
common on reefs. ▼

Angular Triton   6" ▶
Cymatium femorale L.
Caribbean

THE TUN AND FIG SHELLS

These are large, thin-shelled, rounded snails (family Tonnidae), mostly tropical. The animal is usually larger than the shell itself. Adults do not have an operculum but may have a thin, flaky periostracum. The snout contains acid.

Partridge Tun 4″
Tonna perdix L. Indo-Pacific
(The similar *Tonna maculosa*
Dill. is from the ▼
Caribbean.)

▲
Giant Tun 5-7″
Tonna galea L.
World-wide; tropical

Grinning Tun 4-7″
Malea ringens Swain.
Panama (Pacific side)

▲
Atlantic Fig Shell 4″
Ficus communis Röd.
S.E. United States
No operculum

THE MUREX SHELLS

This is a major marine family (Muricidae) which contains a large number of genera and a vast array of species. They are world-wide in distribution, but are found mainly in tropical waters. Long spines and frills characterize this attractive group. The typical *Murex* genus shown on this page contains about 20 species. The operculum is horny.

◄ **Troschel's Murex 5-7"**
Murex troscheli Lisch.
Southeast Asia and Japan

Venus Comb Murex 4-6"
Murex pecten Lightfoot
Indo-Pacific ▼

◄ **Cabrit's Murex 2-3"**
Murex cabriti Bern.
Florida and West Indies

MUREX SHELLS **71**

MUREX SNAILS (below) are large, showy species living colonially on sandy mud flats on the Pacific side of Central America. Many other smaller, attractive species are known in this area. All Murex Snails feed on other mollusks, especially bivalves. Eggs are laid in clusters of capsules.

Radix Murex 4"
Murex radix Gmelin

Pink-mouthed Murex 4"
Murex erythrostomus Swainson

Cabbage Murex 5"
Murex brassica Lamarck

Regal Murex 4"
Murex regius Wood

Earliest use of Murex snails as a source of dye goes back to the days of the Phoenicians. Later, Greeks and Romans made use of the valuable coloring material. The Murex snails secrete a yellowish fluid which, when boiled and treated, makes a permanent purple dye. Wool and cotton dyed with this so-called Royal Tyrian Purple brought very high prices. During Roman times only Senators and Emperors were allowed to wear purple cloth. After the fall of the Roman Empire the dye was used by the Christian Church and gave rise to the official colors of Cardinals. Many new towns were settled in the western Mediterranean by Phoenicians seeking fresh beds of the dye-producing Murex shells.

Boiling
purple dye

Dye Murex 3"
Murex brandaris L.
Mediterranean

INDO-PACIFIC MUREX SHELLS of shallow water include the common species illustrated below. The Endive and Adustus are from coral reefs; Snipe's Bill Murex is from deeper water and occurs in pairs.

Snipe's Bill 4"
Murex haustellum L.

Endive Murex 3"
Murex cichoreus Gmel.

Adustus Murex 2"
Murex brunneus Link

Ramose Murex 8-12"
Murex ramosus L.

SOME RARE MUREX SHELLS

Clavus Murex, rare, may sometimes have a purple mouth. It is more often found in Japan, the Philippines and East Africa. *Murex elongatus* Lightfoot, 2-3½".

The **Zambo Murex** (right) is found on rocks in the central Philippines at depths of 10 ft. *M. zamboi* Burch & Burch. 2".

The **Scorpion Murex** (lower left) may be black, brown or whitish. As it grows, old spines are dissolved by mantle. *Murex scorpio* L. 1-2"

Rose-branch Murex (lower right) is popular collector's item from southeast Asia. *Murex palmarosae* Lam. 3-4".

EASTERN AMERICAN MUREX SHELLS include the common species illustrated below. All live in shallow water, usually on muddy bottoms. All feed on small clams. The Giant Eastern Murex also lives in the Gulf of Mexico. The Apple Murex and Lace Murex are abundant on the west coast of Florida, and are commercially collected.

Rose Murex   2″
M. rubidus F. C. Baker

◄ **Apple Murex   2-4″**
Murex pomum Gmel.

Lace Murex   2½″ ▲
Murex dilectus A. Ads

◄ **Giant Eastern Murex   5″**
Murex fulvescens Sby.
Carolinas to Texas

LATIAXIS SHELLS are abundant and varied in the waters around Japan, which are famous for these species. All are noted for their alabaster white shells and delicate sculpturing. Mawe's Latiaxis, discovered in the early 19th century, was once a great rarity. Now it is more common, and Pilsbry's Latiaxis is considered the top species for collectors. Less attractive species occur in the Caribbean and the Eastern Pacific.

Eugenia's Latiaxis   2"
Latiaxis eugeniae Bern.
Japan; deep water

Armored Latiaxis   1'
Latiaxis armatus Sby.
Japan; deep water

Japan Latiaxis   2"
Latiaxis japonicus Dkr.
Japan; deep water

Mawe's Latiaxis   2½" ▶
Latiaxis mawae G. & P.
Japan; deep water

Pilsbry's Latiaxis   1½"
Latiaxis pilsbryi Hirase
Japan; deep water
▼

ROCK SHELLS of many species (family Thaididae) live in large colonies along rocky shores, where they feed on mussels, oysters and barnacles. Many secrete a purple dye, used by Central American Indians to color cotton. The Barnacle Rock Shell resembles an abalone but has no holes; it is fished commercially for food.

W. Indian Purpura 3″
Purpura patula L.
Florida-Caribbean

Eye of Judas 3″
Purpura picta Perry
Galapagos Islands;
Central America

E. Indian Purpura 3
Purpura persica L.
East Indies

Girdled Rock Shell 1½″
Thais cingulata L.
Cape of Good Hope

Barnacle Rock Shell 4″
Concholepas concholepas Brug.
Peru and Chile

DRUPE SNAILS are small, colorful Thaids found only on the coral-rock shores of the Indo-Pacific area. The Frilled Dogwinkle, common along the northwest shores of North America, has relatives in other cool-water areas such as New England and northern Europe. All members of this family lay urn-like egg capsules.

Prickly Drupe   1"
Drupa ricinus L.

Purple Drupe   1"
Drupa morum Röd.

Finger Drupe   1"
D. grossularia Röd.

Frilled Dogwinkle   1-5" *Nucella lamellosa* Gmel.
N.W. United States; variable in shape and color

▼

Pacific Horse Chestnut   2"
Thais hippocastanea L.
Indo-Pacific

Sertum Rock Shell   2"
Nassa serta Brug.
Indo-Pacific

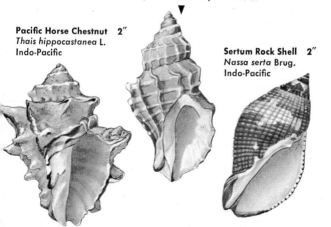

RAPA AND CORAL SNAILS of the family Magilidae are usually closely associated with soft and hard corals or sea fans. Most species do not have radular teeth. The Magilus Snail of the tropical Pacific lives in brain coral. As the coral grows, the snail also lengthens its shell and fills up its early whorls with solid, shelly material. The Papery Rapa lives in soft, yellow corals of the Philippines, maintaining contact with the ocean's water through a small hole in its host. The Caribbean Coral Snail lives in the base of sea fans.

sea fan

snails in base

Caribbean Coral Snails

Caribbean Coral Snail 1"
Coralliophila caribaea Abbott
West Indies

Magilus Snail 1-3"
Magilus antiquus Montfort
Indo-Pacific

Papery Rapa 3"
Rapa rapa L.
Indo-Pacific; lives in soft coral

early whorls

coral

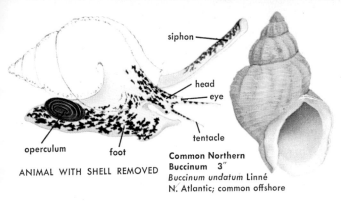

siphon

head

eye

tentacle

operculum   foot

ANIMAL WITH SHELL REMOVED

Common Northern Buccinum 3"
Buccinum undatum Linné
N. Atlantic; common offshore

WHELKS of the family Buccinidae form a large group of many genera and over 400 species. All have corneous opercula and a radula with three rows of strong teeth. Eggs are laid in large clumps of egg capsules. Whelks feed upon marine worms and clams. It is one of the few families to have representatives in both arctic and tropical waters. Arctic species of the genus *Buccinum* are generally drab-colored. The tropical genera are colorful and live in shallow water.

New England Neptune 4"
Neptunea decemcostata Say
Canada to Mass.; common offshore

Neptune egg capsules

COLD WATER WHELKS

The Buccinids are ravenous carnivores, and the larger species do great damage to clam beds. In Japan, they are commercially fished for food and are used as bait. Species like the Japelion are common in fossil beds and indicate cold-water conditions in former geological times. A few species of Buccinids may lack an operculum. The cold-water Buccinids are few in species but numerous as individuals, but in the tropics are colorful and varied.

◄ **Hirase's Whelk   4"**
Japelion hirasei Pils.
Northern Japan; a cold-water species

Dilated Whelk   6-7" ►
Penion dilatatus Q. & G.
New Zealand;
a cold-water species

operculum

TROPICAL WHELKS

Spiral Babylon 3"
Babylonia spirata L.
S.E. Asia

Signum Whelk 2"
Siphonalia signum Reeve
A common species in Japan;
a pest of oysters.

False Triton 3"
Colubraria maculosa Gmelin
Indian Ocean; an uncommon
species found around coral reefs.

Zelandic Babylon 3"
B. zelandica Bruguière
Indian Ocean; uncommon
Note the purple ridge at
the base of the shell.

Phos Whelk 2"
Phos senticosus Linné
Indo-Pacific; commonly dredged

Channeled Babylon 2"
B. canaliculata Schumacher
Indian Ocean

THE MELONGENAS (Melongenidae) are carnivores, feeding on clams and snails. The Australian Trumpet is the world's largest gastropod—over two feet long. The young hatch from the egg capsule with a long, slender spire which is usually broken off by the time the animals mature.

American Crown Conch   2-4"
Melongena corona Gmelin
S.E. United States; common

◄ **Australian Trumpet or Baler   2 ft.**
Syrinx aruanus L.
N. Australia

Caribbean Crown Conch   4-5"
Melongena melongena L.
West Indies; found in shallow
water; feeds on clams.

young shell of
Australian Trumpet

TULIP SHELLS (Fasciolariidae) are typical of S.E. United States. Three species in Florida include the 20-inch Horse Conch. Tulips lay their eggs in large clumps of parchment-like capsules. Adults feed on clams.

Banded Tulip 3"
Fasciolaria hunteria Perry
Carolinas to Texas; feed on clams

Florida Horse Conch 20" ▶
Pleuroploca gigantea Kiener
Carolinas to Mexico

True Tulip 4-6" ▼
Fasciolaria tulipa Linné
Carolinas to West Indies; common

operculum of Tulip

young shell of Horse Conch

operculum

Closter Spindle   7"
Fusinus closter Philippi
Lower Caribbean; uncommon

Distaff Spindle   4"
Fusinus colus Linné
Indo-Pacific

Nicobar Spindle   4" ▶
F. nicobaricus Lamarck
Indo-Pacific

SPINDLE SHELLS form a genus *(Fusinus)* of some 50 species, well known to collectors because of their long, graceful shape. These snails live on sandy bottoms and travel in pairs. The largest Atlantic species, the Closter Spindle, is a collectors' item.

FULGUR WHELKS (genus *Busycon*) of eastern American waters have been abundant since Miocene times, some 30 million years ago. Today there are six common species. Long chains of egg capsules are often washed ashore. The Lightning Whelk is normally "left-handed."

a string of egg cases

Knobbed Whelk 7"
Busycon carica Gmelin
Mass. to Georgia

Channeled Whelk 6"
B. canaliculatum Linné
Mass. to Florida ▶

Lightning Whelk 4-16"
Busycon contrarium Conrad
Carolinas to Texas ◀

Living Olive Shell showing extended parts

OLIVE SHELLS (family Olividae) with their agate-like sheen and attractive shape have long been favorites. The family is characterized by great variation in color and markings. The genus *Oliva* has no operculum. The mantle and foot of the living animals cover the outer shell. Over 300 species of Olive Shells live on sandy bottoms where they feed on smaller mollusks. The best time to collect Olives is at night, at low tide. Philippine collectors use bait on a tiny hook and line.

Ear Olive   2"
Olivancillaria auricularia
Lamarck
Eastern South America

◄ **Tent Olive   3-5"**
Oliva porphyria L.
W. Central America

Tankerville's Olive   3"
Ancilla tankervillei Swain.
Venezuela

Orange-mouthed Olive   3″ *Oliva sericea* Röding
Indo-Pacific. Note color variation on backs.
This is a very common sand dwelling species.

Purple-mouthed Olive   2-3″
Oliva episcopalis Lamarck
Indo-Pacific; common

Gibbose Olive   2″
Oliva gibbosa Röding
Indian Ocean; abundant

Lettered Olive   2½″ ▶
Oliva sayana Ravenel
S.E. United States; common in sand

VASE SHELLS

About two dozen species (family Vasidae), all tropical, have heavy shells with 4 to 5 spiral ridges on the inner lip. Most are common and found near shore, but some, like the Latirus-shaped Vase, are deep-water species.

Common Atlantic Vase   4"
Vasum muricatum Born
Florida and West Indies
A common inshore species.

Latirus-shaped Vase   2"
V. latiriforme Reh. & Abb.
Gulf of Mexico; rare ▶

Ceram Vase   4-5"
V. ceramicum Linné
Indo-Pacific
A common reef species.
▼

Pacific Top Vase   3"
V. turbinellus L.
Indo-Pacific; common

Globe Vase   1"
V. globulus Lam.
Lesser Antilles
Uncommon

CHANK SHELLS

The very massive Chank Shells (Turbinellidae) are found in only a few areas. In India and Ceylon they are collected by the thousands and cut into ornamental rings and bangles. Rare "left-handed" specimens are mounted in gold and placed on Hindu altars. Chanks are characterized by a nipple-like apex and folds on the inner lip.

West Indian Chank   10″
Turbinella angulata Ltft.
Bahamas, Cuba and Mexico
A common shallow-water
species in the Bahamas.
Outer skin flakes off.

◄ **Indian Chank   6″**
Turbinella pyrum L.
Bay of Bengal, India

MITER SHELLS

The renowned Mitridae family of warm, shallow seas includes nearly 600 species, from 0.3 to 6 in. long. The inner lip usually has 3 to 5 strong, curved teeth. Miters use their long retractable snout to feed on worms and clams. They burrow in sand but keep their siphon extended. Eggs, in small horny capsules, are attached to stones. The Indo-Pacific region has about 400 species of Miters. Some of the larger and more common ones are illustrated on these two pages. Miters are usually found under rocks.

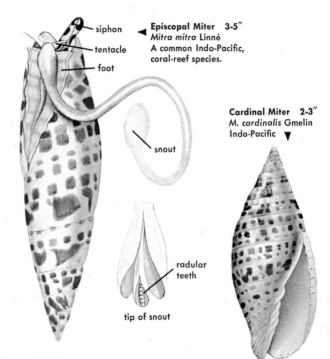

siphon

tentacle

foot

Episcopal Miter   3-5"
Mitra mitra Linné
A common Indo-Pacific,
coral-reef species.

snout

Cardinal Miter   2-3"
M. cardinalis Gmelin
Indo-Pacific ▼

radular
teeth

tip of snout

Adusta Miter
Mitra eremitarum Röding

Pin-pointed Miter 2″
M. puncticulata Lamarck

Pontifical Miter 2″
M. stictica Link

Papal Miter 3-4″ *M. papalis* Linné ▶
One of the handsomest of the uncommon
Miters from the Indo-Pacific area.

INDO-PACIFIC
MITERS

Imperial Miter 2″
M. imperialis Röding
▼

Melon-like Miter 1″
M. cucumerina Lamarck

Plicate Miter 2"
Vexillum plicarium L.
Indo-Pacific; common

Rugose Miter 2"
V. rugosum L.
Indo-Pacific; common

Little Fox Miter 2"
V. vulpeculum L.
Indo-Pacific; common

▲
Belcher's Miter 3"
Mitra belcheri Hinds
West Panama; uncommon

Zaca Miter 3"
M. zaca Strong & Hanna
West Panama; uncommon
▼

Barbados Miter 2"
M. barbadensis Gmel.
Caribbean; common

Nodulose Miter 2"
M. nodulosa Gmel.
Caribbean; common

COMMON INDO-PACIFIC MITERS

Letter Miter ¾″
Mitra litterata Lam.

Papilio Miter 2″
M. papilio Link

Isabel Miter 3″
M. isabella Swains.

Auger-like Miter 4″
M. terebralis Lamarck

Poor Miter 1″
M. paupercula L.

Blood-sucker Miter 2″
M. sanguisuga L.

Sino Miter 1½″
Pterygia sinensis Rve.
East Asia

Nucea Miter 2″
Pterygia nucea Gmel.
Indo-Pacific

Dactylus Miter 2′
Pterygia dactylus L.
Indo-Pacific

Casta Miter 2″
Swainsonia casta Gmelin
Indo-Pacific

Olive-shaped Miter ½-¾″
Swainsonia olivaeformis Swain.
Indo-Pacific

Cone Miter 1″
Pterygia conus Gmel.
Southwest Pacific

Common Imbricaria ¾″
Imbricaria conica Schum.
South Pacific

Fenestrate Miter ' ¾″
Pterygia fenestrata Lam.
Indo-Pacific

Some of the smaller species of Miter Shells (above) show
great diversity in shape, especially Indo-Pacific genera
such as *Swainsonia*, *Imbricaria* and *Pterygia*. Some of
these strange Miters resemble Cones, Olives and *Strombus* Conchs. These genera contain only a few dozen species which are all sand-dwellers.

VOLUTES

Volute shells (Volutidae) are large, colorful gastropods. Popular with collectors, some command high prices. Of about 200 kinds, most live in shallow, tropical seas, but some come from deep waters and a few from polar waters. Volutes are carnivorous, rapid crawlers. Females lay eggs in leathery capsules. The operculum is absent in most, but not in the true *Voluta*. Volute shells have strong folds, fairly constant in number, on the columnella.

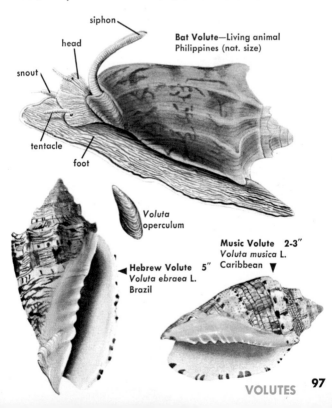

siphon

head

snout

tentacle

foot

Bat Volute—Living animal
Philippines (nat. size)

Voluta
operculum

◄ **Hebrew Volute 5"**
Voluta ebraea L.
Brazil

Music Volute 2-3"
Voluta musica L.
Caribbean ▼

Bat Volute 3"
Aulica vespertilio Linné
Indo-Pacific; common

Aulica Volute 4"
Aulica aulica Ltft. ▶
Philippines; rare

◀ **Noble Volute** 5"
Aulica nobilis Lightfoot
S.E. Asia; uncommon

Imperial Volute 10"
Aulica imperialis Lightfoot
Philippines; uncommon
▼

FLORIDA VOLUTES belong to the subfamily Scaphellinae, and all live in fairly deep water except for the Junonia, which is occasionally washed ashore in west Florida. The animals are spotted like their shells and they all lack an operculum. Some are very rare.

Kiener's Volute 4-7" ▶
Scaphella kieneri Clench
Deep water; rare

▲
Dohrn's Volute 3"
Scaphella dohrni Sby.
Deep water; rare

Junonia Volute 4-5" ▶
Scaphella junonia Shaw
S.E. United States

JAPANESE VOLUTES

Shin-bone Volute 2½"
Teramachia tibiaeformis Kuroda
Japan; rare

Asian Flame Volute 4" ▶
Fulgoraria rupestris Gmel.
China and Formosa

◀ **Notable Japanese Volute** 5"
Fulgoraria concinna Brod.
Japan

Delicate Volute 3" ▲
Fulgoraria delicata Fulton
Japan

VOLUTES

Lightning Volute 5″ ►
Ericusa fulgetrum Sby.
South Australia

Vexillate Volute 3″ ▲
Harpulina arausiaca Lightfoot
Ceylon

Arab Volute 4″
Alcithoe arabica Gmelin
New Zealand ►

Ponsonby's Volute 2″ ▲
Alcithoe ponsonbyi E. A. Smith
South Africa

MELON OR BALER SHELLS

◄ **Mammal Volute 10″**
Livonia mammilla Sowerby
South Australia

▲
Indian Volute 8″
Melo melo Ltft.
Southeast Asia

Ethiopian Volute 6-14″
Melo aethiopicus Linné ►
Indo-Pacific

▲
**Elephant's Snout
Volute 10-14"**
Cymbium cymbium L.

Olla Volute 8" ▲
Cymbium philipinum Röding

Neptune's Volute 6" ▶
Cymbium pepo Lightfoot

AUSTRALIAN VOLUTES

Turner's Volute 2"
Amoria turneri Gray
N. Australia
▼

Elliot's Volute 3"
Amoria ellioti Sby.
South Australia

Damon's Volute ◄
Amoria damoni Gr
Western Australia

◄ **Bednall's Volute 4"**
Volutoconus bednalli Brazier
Northern Australia; rare

Gross' Volute 4½" ►
Volutoconus grossi Iredale
Queensland; rare

Some Volutes not only have a very broad foot, but also extend the fleshy, shell-making mantle over the outer shell, such as seen in the top view of a crawling Angular Volute from Brazil (left).

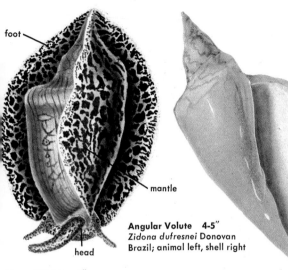

foot

mantle

head

Angular Volute 4-5"
Zidona dufresnei Donovan
Brazil; animal left, shell right

Abyssal Volute 3"
Volutocorbis abyssicola Ads. & Rve.
South Africa; deep water

Delessert's Volute 2" ▶
Lyria delessertiana Petit
Madagascar

Miter-shaped Volute 2"
Lyria mitraeformis Lam.
South Australia

NUTMEGS (Cancellariidae) are oddly sculptured with strong spiral teeth on the inner lip. The largest number of species are in the western American tropics.

Cancellate Nutmeg 1″
Cancellaria cancellata L.
West Africa
Moderately common.

Oblique Nutmeg 1″
C. obliquata Lam.
Indo-Pacific
Commonly dredged.

Yellow-mouthed Nutmeg 1″
C. chrysostoma Sby.
West Central America
Uncommon offshore; mouth sometimes orange, but fades when shell is dead.

► **Spengler's Nutmeg** 2″
C. spengleriana Desh.
East Asia; common

Common Nutmeg 2″
C. reticulata L.
S.E. United States

Helmet-shaped Nutmeg 1½″
C. cassidiformis Sby.
Panama to Ecuador

MARGIN SHELLS (Marginellidae) are small and colorful, especially those from the shores of West Africa. Bubble Margin is the largest of about 100 species.

**Common Atlantic
Margin Shell** ⅓"
Prunum apicinum Mke.
U.S. to Caribbean
Common in bays

**Orange Margin
Shell** 1"
Prunum carneum Stor.
Florida-Caribbean
Uncommon offshore.

**Rose Margin
Shell** 1"
Marginella rosea Lam.
South Africa
Uncommon offshore.

Bubble Margin Shell 2-3"
Prunum bullatum Born
Brazil; uncommon

Belted Margin Shell 1"
Prunum cingulatum Dillwyn
West Africa

Bean Margin Shell 1"
Marginella faba Linné
West Africa

CONE SHELLS

Cone Shells (Conidae) total about 400 species from most warm, tropical waters. The majority of the species are Indo-Pacific. Some 50 species are found in the Americas and over a hundred fossil species are known. Cones are heavy, with broad spires and tapering whorls, although some are as small as a grain of rice. Cones are carnivorous, feeding on worms and small fish. A few from the Indian and Pacific oceans can inflict serious and perhaps fatal stings. The largest of the Textile Cones and the Indo-Pacific Geography Cones are venomous. Poison from the venom sac in the head and a tiny "harpoon" in the radula sac are ejected from the proboscis and stabbed into the victim. Cones prefer shallow water in coral reefs and under rocks. Their eggs, in flat, leaf-like capsules, are attached to rocks.

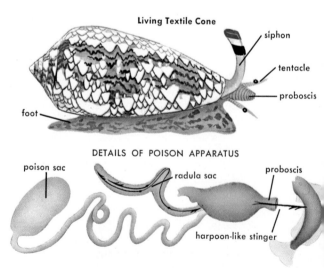

Living Textile Cone

siphon

tentacle

proboscis

foot

DETAILS OF POISON APPARATUS

poison sac

radula sac

proboscis

harpoon-like stinger

GLORY-OF-THE-SEAS

This cone shell, *Conus gloria-maris* Chemnitz, 4-5 in. long, is considered the most valuable shell in the world. Only 70 specimens have ever been found, perfect ones selling for $1,200. In the Philippines and Indonesia, every collector hopes to stumble on a colony of them. So far, only one or two have been found at one time. Note the almost straight, graceful outlines of the whorls and the fine network of coloration. Do not confuse this with the common Textile Cones shown on page 113. Their sides are much more rounded and their spires less elevated. The Glory-of-the-Seas has not been known to be fatal, but is probably capable of inflicting a serious sting. Most known specimens are in natural history museums.

COMMON INDO-PACIFIC CONES

dark phase

light phase

Eburneus Cone   2"
Conus eburneus Hwass
Two color forms

Fig Cone   3"
Conus figulinus Linné
Right: with periostracum
Left: cleaned shell

Tessellate Cone   1-2"
Conus tessulatus Born
Spots vary in size.

Marble Cone   4"
Conus marmoreus Linné
Rarely albinistic

Leopard Cone 5-9"
Conus leopardus Röding
Note white lower end.

Pacific Lettered Cone 3-5"
Conus litteratus L.
Note brownish end.

The common Indo-Pacific Cones on these two pages live in sand, usually near coral reefs. By day they hide in the sand; at night they emerge and feed—mainly on marine worms. Living shell has a "skin" or periostracum.

Betulinus Cone. *Conus betulinus* L.
Southwest Pacific **4-6"**

Hebrew Cone ½-1½"
Conus ebraeus Linné
Indian and Pacific oceans

Nussatella Cone 3″
Conus nussatella Linné
Indo-Pacific reefs

Distant Cone 4″
Conus distans Hwass.
Indo-Pacific reefs

Virgin Cone 4″
Conus virgo Linné
Indo-Pacific bays

Magus Cone 3″
Conus magus Linné
Indo-Pacific
A variable species

Soldier Cone 3″
Conus miles Linné
Indo-Pacific

two color forms

TEXTILE CONES

This group of cone shells, found mainly in the Indo-Pacific region, is marked with small tent-like triangles. All are closely related to the common Textile Cone (right). The large ones are venomous. See Glory-of-the-Seas, page 109.

◄ **Netted Cone   2″**
Conus retifer Menke
Indo-Pacific; uncommon

Textile Cone   3-4″ ►
Conus textile Linné
Indo-Pacific; common

Aulicus Cone   4-6″
Conus aulicus Linné
Indo-Pacific; uncommon
▼

Queen Victoria Cone   3″
Conus victoriae Reeve
N.W. Australia

Abbas Cone   3″
Conus abbas Hwass
Indo-Pacific
Uncommon

The cones on this page are unusual and the pride of collectors. The Geography Cone is venomous, the General is the most common, and the Pertusa is hardest to find.

Pertusa Cone 1½"
Conus pertusus Hwass
Indo-Pacific

Lithograph Cone 2"
Conus litoglyphus Hwass
Indo-Pacific

Pontifical Cone 1"
Conus dorreensis
Péron and Lesueur
Australia

Bough Cone 4"
Conus thalassiarchus Sby.
Philippines; uncommon

General Cone 3"
Conus generalis L.
Indo-Pacific
Variable colors
▼

Geography Cone 5"
Conus geographus Linné
Indo-Pacific

These cones are so rare that few collectors have them all. Their rarity may indicate that their true habitat, where they may be more common, has not been discovered.

Rhododendron Cone 2¼"
Conus adamsoni Broderip
Central Pacific

Bubble Cone   2-3"
Conus bullatus Linné
Western Pacific

Nobility Cone   1-2"
Conus nobilis Linné
Southwest Pacific; rare
in most areas, but less so
in the Sulu Sea, Philippines.

Zoned Cone   3"
Conus zonatus Hwass
Andaman Islands

Cancellate Cone 1½″
Conus cancellatus Hwass

Deep Sea Cone 3″
Conus profundorum Kuroda
Rare

Teramachi's Cone 3″
Conus teramachi Kuroda
Rare; deep water

JAPANESE CONES

Austral Cone 3″
Conus australis Holten

Siebold's Cone 3″
Conus sieboldi Reeve

Fulmen Cone 2″
Conus fulmen Reeve
Shallow water; common

WEST AFRICAN CONES

Genuanus Cone 2″
Conus genuanus Linné
Rare

Trader Cone 1½″
Conus mercator Linné
Uncommon

Prometheus Cone 8-12″
Conus prometheus Hwass
Largest living cone

Butterfly Cone 3″ ▶
C. papilionaceus Hwass
Common

FLORIDA-CARIBBEAN CONES

Crown Cone   3″ ◀
Conus regius Gmelin
Common on reefs
S. Fla.-W. Indies

Alphabet Cone   3″ ▶
Conus spurius Gmelin
Common in sand
Fla.-Gulf of Mex.

Jeweled Cone   ½″ ◀
Conus armillatus C. B. Ads.
Caribbean; rare

Florida Cone   2″ ▶
Conus floridanus Gabb
Common in sand
N. Car.-Florida; variable

Glory-of-the-Atlantic   2″ ◀
Conus granulatus L.
Florida-W. Indies; rare

Sozon's Cone   4″ ▶
Conus sozoni Bartsch
Southeast U.S.
Uncommon offshore

Interrupted Cone 2″
Conus ximenes Gray
Mexico to Peru

PACIFIC PANAMA CONES

Ladder Cone 2″ ▲
Conus scalaris Valenciennes
Gulf of California

Lucid Cone 2″
Conus lucidus Wood
Mexico to Ecuador

Prince Cone 2½″
Conus princeps Linné
Mexico to Ecuador

Pear-shaped Cone 3″
Conus patricius Hinds
Nicaragua to Ecuador

AUGER SHELLS (Terebridae) are long and brightly colored. The radula and poison gland are similar to those of Cone Shells. No venomous sting has been recorded. Most are tropical sand-dwellers. The largest of some 300 species is the Indo-Pacific Marlinspike, 6-8 inches long.

◄ **Strigate Auger** 1½″
Terebra strigillata Linné
Indo-Pacific; uncommon

◄ **Duplicate Auger** 3″
Terebra duplicata Lamarck
Australia; common in
sand in shallow water.

foot

eye
tentacle
mouth

Marlinspike 6-10″
Terebra maculata Linné
Indo-Pacific; abundant

Tiger Auger 2″
Terebra felina Dill.
Indo-Pacific; common

COMMON INDO-PACIFIC AUGERS

Subulate Auger 6″
Terebra subulata Linné
Indo-Pacific; sandy areas
▼

Muscaria Auger 6″
Terebra areolata Link
Indo-Pacific; near reefs
▼

operculum of
Subulate Auger

▲
Dimidiate Auger 6″
Terebra dimidiata Linné
Indo-Pacific; muddy sand

◄ Triseriate Auger   5"
Terebra triseriata Gray
Indo-Pacific; collector's item

enlarged
section

Crenulata Auger   6"
Terebra crenulata L.
Indo-Pacific; common
Left: typical form
Right: *fimbriata* form

▲

Eyed Auger   6"
Terebra guttata Röding
Indo-Pacific; uncommon

122   AUGERS

INDO-PACIFIC AUGERS

1. Cerithina Auger 1″
Terebra cerithina Lam.
Common

2. Chlorate Auger 2″
Terebra chlorata Lam.
Common

3. Affinis Auger 1″
Terebra affinis Gray
Abundant. Lives in sand, under rocks

4. Babylon Auger 1″
Terebra babylonia Lam.
Abundant. Lives in sand, under rocks

These small Augers live in sand at depths of 3 to 60 feet. They take shelter under small coral rocks. Collectors "fan" the water briskly to stir away the sand and reveal the brightly colored Augers. Some people use wire-mesh sieves.

Nebulose Auger 3″
Terebra nebulosa Sby.
Uncommon; in sand

Lance Auger 2″
Terebra lanceata L.
Uncommon; in sand

FLORIDA-CARIBBEAN AUGERS

1. Gray Auger 3/4"
Terebra cinerea Gmelin
West Indies; common

2. Atlantic Auger 2"
Terebra dislocata Say
S.E. United States; common

3. Florida Auger 3"
Terebra floridana Dall
Off Florida; uncommon

4. Flame Auger 4-6"
Terebra taurinus Lightfoot
A rare West Indian species

5. Shiny Auger 2"
Terebra hastata Gmelin
Florida-West Indies

CENTRAL AMERICAN AUGERS

1. Variegate Auger 2″
Terebra variegata Gray
Panama; moderately common

2. Robust Auger 4″
Terebra robusta Hinds
Mexico to Ecuador; uncommon

3. Zebra Auger 4″
Terebra strigata Sby.
Mexico to Panama; uncommon

In sandy areas between Lower Calif. and Ecuador about 40 species of *Terebra* are found. A few are outstanding in color and size; most are small; some very common. These three burrow in muddy sand.

TURRID SHELLS (Turridae) are a highly evolved group of marine gastropods. The radular teeth have been reduced to a single row in most forms. Most have a "turrid" notch or indentation on the upper part of the outer lip. Several hundred species of variable shapes are found both in very deep and in shallow water. Turrid Shells vary

Humped Turrid 2″
Crassispira gibbosa Ba
West Indies

Fusiform Turrid 3″
Spergo fusiforme Kur. & Habe
Japan; rare

Babylon Turrid 3″
Turris babylonia Linné
Indo-Pacific; common

Ear Turrid 1″
Turris auriculifera Lamarck
Indo-Pacific; common

in length from 1/16 to 5". The Japanese Thatcheria, below, is the world's largest Turrid Shell. A few cold-water species are sinistrally coiled, or "left-handed." Japan alone has over 400 species of Turrids.

top view

JAPANESE TURRIDS

face view

Miraculous Thatcheria   4-5"
Thatcheria mirabilis Sby.
Japan; deep water

Left-handed Turrid   2"
Antiplanes contraria Yokoyama
Bering Sea

◀ **Dall's Aforia   3"**
Aforia circinata Dall
Japan

head

tentacle

foot

Living Paper Bubble

Paper Bubble 2"; *Hydatina physis* L. Indo-Pacific

BUBBLE SHELLS (order Tectibranchia) have external, plume-like gills and both sexes present in the same individual. Some have internal shells, but those of the Bubble Shell family (Bullidae) are external, large, and spacious. Bubble Shells, mostly tropical, are carnivorous. They lay eggs in long, gelatinous strands.

Atlantic Bulla 1½"
Bulla striata Bruguière
West Indies; abundant

White-banded Bubble 1"
Hydatina albocincta Hoeven
Japan; uncommon

Amplustre Bubble 1½"
Aplustrum amplustre Linné
Indo-Pacific; uncommon

Pacific Bubble 2"
Bulla ampulla Linné
Indo-Pacific; abundant

THE BIVALVES

The pelecypods, or lamellibranchs, the second largest class of mollusks, contain about 10,000 species of bivalves, including the clams, mussels, oysters and scallops. About one third live in fresh water; the others are marine. They lack a head and radular teeth. Feeding is aided by the gills, and most species live on microscopic plant life. The mantle is modified at the posterior end into two tubular siphons which draw and expel water from the mantle cavity. The two shells (valves) are kept closed by strong adductor muscles, and kept slightly open by the action of an elastic, horny pad or ridge—the ligament. Most bivalves shed their eggs directly into the water, but a few brood the young in gill pouches. The sexes may be combined in one individual or may be separate.

Oysters, clams and scallops are a major source of food. From oysters come valuable pearls. The Teredo Shipworm, a bivalve, is destructive to wharf pilings.

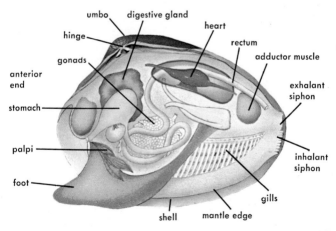

ARK SHELLS (Arcidae) have a long series of small, similar teeth on the hinge. They have no siphons and most are anchored by a byssus of hair-like threads. Of 200 species (24 American) most are tropical; many are gathered commercially for food.

West Indian Turkey Wing 3"
Arca zebra Swainson
Carolinas to W. Indies
and Bermuda

PEN SHELLS (Pinnidae), large and fragile, live buried in soft sand anchored by a silky byssus. Ancients made a "golden fleece" from the byssal threads of Giant Mediterranean Pen, *Pinna nobilis* L., 14 in. (front). The black shell (back) is the American Stiff Pen Shell (*Atrina rigida* Sol. 7 in.).

WING OYSTERS (Pteriidae), edible but unpalatable, seldom produce precious pearls. Tropical species, with pearly interiors and long, wing-like projections of the hinge, have fragile shells. Wing Oysters attach themselves to the ocean bottom and to wharf pilings.

Giant Wing Oyster 7" ▶
Pteria penguin Röding
Indo-Pacific; moderately common

▲   ▶
PEARL OYSTERS, six tropical species, live on rocky ocean bottoms. Layers of calcium carbonate around a foreign body in the mantle make pearls. Most productive are the Black-lipped, above (*Pinctada margaritifera* L., S.E. Asia, 6 in.), and Japanese, right (*P. mertensi* Dunker, 3 in.).

HAMMER OYSTERS
(Isognomonidae)

side view

Flat Tree Oyster 3"
Isognomon alatus Gmelin
Florida and W. Indies; common
Lives in lower mangrove branches

Common Hammer Oyster 4-6"
Malleus malleus Linné
Indo-Pacific; common

White Hammer Oyster 4-7"
Malleus albus Lamarck
Indo-Pacific. Shallow water;
anchors to bottom; common

MUSSELS (Mytilidae) are the most abundant of all mollusks. They occur in dense colonies on rocky shores and wharf pilings. Mussels protect and feed many kinds of snails, worms, and crabs. **File Clams,** (Limidae), swim away from predators by flapping their shells and tentacles. Some File Clams build nests for protection.

Atlantic Ribbed Mussel   3-4"
Modiolus demissus Dillwyn
Lives in marsh peat
Canada to Texas

▶**Blue Edible Mussel   2-3"**
Mytilus edulis Linné
Lives on rocky coasts
Europe and N.E. America

Rough File Clam   2-4"
Lima scabra Born
Florida and W. Indies
Living clam at left

SCALLOPS (Pectinidae) are a world-wide group of several hundred species, including several large northern kinds fished commercially for the large single muscle, which is excellent eating. By snapping their shells together, scallops propel themselves rapidly in a zigzag direction. Most kinds have a series of brightly colored eyes along the edge of the mantle. These are sensitive to minor changes in light intensity, as might be caused by a passing fish. What appear to be the top and bottom valves of the scallop are actually left and right valves. The left (lower) valve is usually more convex.

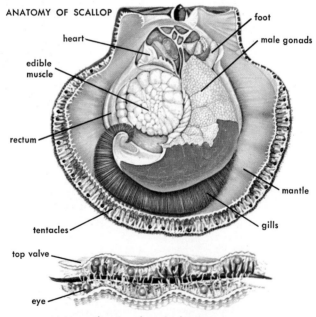

ANATOMY OF SCALLOP

foot
male gonads
heart
edible muscle
rectum
mantle
tentacles
gills
top valve
eye

edge view of mantle, showing eyes

JAPANESE SCALLOPS. These two deep-water species show an unusual range of pastel color variations.

Top Row: **Swift's Scallop 3-5"**, *Chlamys swifti* Bernardi
Bottom Row: **Noble Scallop, 3-5"**, *Chlamys nobilis* Reeve

EASTERN AMERICAN SCALLOPS are found from Labrador to the West Indies. The Calico Scallop, used in shell jewelry, is abundant offshore in south Florida. Lion's Paw, a strong heavy shell, is a collector's favorite. Atlantic Deep Sea and Atlantic Bay Scallops, both common on the East Coast, are popular seafood.

Lion's Paw 3-5"
Lyropecten nodosus Linné
Florida-W. Indies

Calico Scallop 1-2"
Aequipecten gibbus Linné
S.E. U.S.-Caribbean

Atlantic Deep Sea Scallop 8"
Placopecten magellanicus Gmelin
Labrador—Carolinas

Atlantic Bay Scallop 4"
Aequipecten irradians Lamarck
Eastern United States

INDO-PACIFIC SCALLOPS do not compare with other famous shells of this region. Most unusual is large Asian Moon Scallop with bottom valve white, top valve colored.

Leopard Scallop 3"
Annachlamys leopardus Reeve
Northern Australia; uncommon

Mantle Scallop 3"
Gloripallium pallium Linné
Indo-Pacific; common

Asian Moon Scallop 4-5"
Amusium pleuronectes L. ▶
S.E. Asia
Deep water; common

Folded Scallop 2"
Decatopecten plica L.
S.E. Asia

THORNY OYSTERS are not related to true oysters. The huge *Hinnites* of western American waters is in the scallop family and may weigh up to 20 lbs. The Thorny Oysters of the family Spondylidae have a typical ball-and-socket

Giant Rock Scallop   4-8"
Hinnites multirugosus Gale
Alaska to Mexico

adult form

young form

Atlantic Thorny Oyster   6"   *Spondylus americanus* Hermann
Florida and Caribbean; two color forms shown below.

hinge joint and develop long spines. They occur in deep water, usually in the tropics, and have a rich, varied color pattern. These fairly common bivalves are sometimes called Chrysanthemum shells.

Regal Thorny Oyster
5-8"
Spondylus regius L.
S.E. Asia

Pacific Thorny Oyster   3-6"
Spondylus princeps Brod.
Mexico to Panama

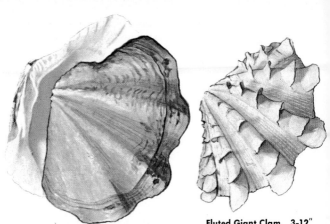

Giant Clam   2-4 ft.
Tridacna gigas Linné
Indo-Pacific

Fluted Giant Clam   3-12"
Tridacna squamosa Lam.
Indo-Pacific

GIANT CLAM (Tridacnidae) is the largest shelled mollusk, exceeded only by the 55-ft. Giant Squid of the N. Atlantic. It is not a man-eating clam. The Giant Clam of Indo-Pacific coral reefs feeds on colonies of marine algae which grow in its fleshy mantle. A non-precious pearl the size of a golf ball may be produced.

Giant Clam in coral reef.
Color of mantle varies.

JEWEL BOXES (Chamidae), about 20 species of them, live attached to rocks and wrecks. These tropical shells are variable in form and brilliantly colored.

CARDITAS, also from tropical waters, are long and radially ribbed. They are common clams of shallow, muddy bays. About 30 species have been recorded.

Lazarus Jewel Box   4"
Chama lazarus Linné
Indo-Pacific

Leafy Jewel Box   3"
Chama macerophylla Gmelin
Fla. and Caribbean

Rosy Cardita   2"
Cardita crassicosta Lam.
Australia; uncommon

Broad-ribbed Cardita   1-1½"
Cardita floridana Con.
Florida; abundant

CHAMAS AND CARDITAS   **141**

LUCINES (Lucinidae) are world-wide tropical clams with strong, thin shells and long anterior muscle scars. The two siphons are very short; the hinge may be well toothed or toothless. Most of the 200 species are eaten by fishes but a few are used as food by man. The Elegant Fimbria is a delicately formed and tinted relative.

pallial line

anterior muscle scar

Thick Lucine 2"
Phacoides pectinata Gmelin
Fla. to Caribbean; common

Buttercup Lucine 2"
Anodontia alba Link
S.E. U.S.-Caribbean; abundant

Pennsylvania Lucine 2"
Lucina pensylvanica L.
S.E. U.S.-Caribbean; common

Pacific Tiger Lucine 5″
Codakia tigerina Linné
Indo-Pacific; abundant

Punctate Lucine 3″
Codakia punctata Linné
Indo-Pacific; common

Elegant Fimbria 3″
Fimbria soverbii Reeve
S.W. Pacific; rare

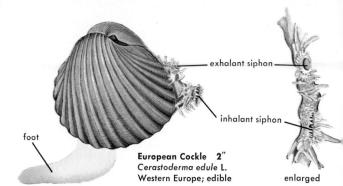

exhalant siphon

inhalant siphon

foot

European Cockle 2″
Cerastoderma edule L.
Western Europe; edible

enlarged

COCKLES (Cardiidae) are a large group of colorful species which demonstrate an evolutionary explosion, the result of which is an array of bizarre shapes showing all degrees of sculpturing. Some species are copious and ribbed; others are compressed. Cockles are active animals. They can jump several inches by means of a long, powerful foot. A current of water entering through the inhalant siphon brings food and a supply of oxygen. Cockles are a food for fishes as well as for man.

Costate Cockle 4″
Cardium costatum Linné
West Africa; uncommon

Prickly Cockle 2″
Trachycardium egmontianum Shutt.
S.E. U.S.; common in sand
Sometimes pure white (albinistic)

Lyrate Cockle 2″
Discors lyrata Sby.
S.E. Asia; uncommon

Heart Cockle 3″
Corculum cardissa Linné
Indo-Pacific; common

Oblong Cockle 2″
Laevicardium oblongum Gm.
Europe; uncommon

Half-heart Cockle 1½″ ▶
Hemicardium hemicardium L.
Indo-Pacific; uncommon

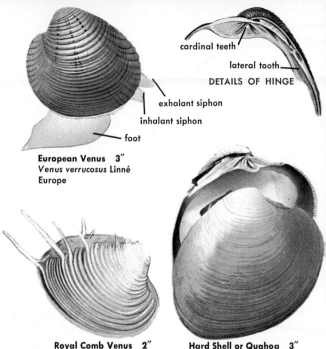

cardinal teeth

lateral tooth

DETAILS OF HINGE

exhalant siphon

inhalant siphon

foot

European Venus 3"
Venus verrucosus Linné
Europe

Royal Comb Venus 2"
Pitar dione Linné
Tex. to Carib.; uncommon

Hard Shell or Quahog 3"
Mercenaria mercenaria Linné
Eastern U.S.; edible

VENUS CLAMS (Veneridae) are probably the most successful of all the clams. Over 400 abundant species occur the world over. All have hinges which bear interlocking lateral and cardinal teeth. The well-developed foot is compressed and hatchet-shaped. American Indians once manufactured their wampum from the Quahog, the chief commercial clam of east coastal U.S. Young Quahogs are known as cherrystones and littlenecks. The Philippines have over one hundred varieties of Venus Clams.

Calico Clam 2″
Macrocallista maculata L.
Carolinas to Caribbean
Introduced to Bermuda

Pismo Clam 5″
Tivela stultorum Mawe
Calif. to Mexico

King Venus 1½″ ▶
Chione paphia Linné
West Indies; uncommon

Sunray Venus 5″
Macrocallista nimbosa Lightfoot
S.E. United States; common
▼

VENUS CLAMS **147**

INDO-PACIFIC VENUS CLAMS

Wedding Cake Venus 2½"
Callanaitis disjecta Perry
Australia; uncommon

Lamellate Venus 2"
Antigona lamellaris Schum.
Indo-Pacific; common

Golden Venus 3"
Paphia euglypta Phil.
East Asia; uncommon

Squamose Venus 1"
Anomalodiscus squamosus L.
S.E. Asia; common

exterior

interior

◄ **Lettered Venus 3"**
Tapes literata Linné
Indo-Pacific; common

TELLINS (Tellinidae) are a large, mainly tropical, family of sand-dwelling clams with elongate fragile shells and two long, separate siphons. Over 200 species; most are shiny and delicately tinted. The Sunrise Tellin is used in shell-jewelry manufacture.

Candy Stick Tellin 1″
Tellina similis Sby.
Fla.-Caribbean; abundant

siphon

foot

Hatchet Tellin 1″
Tellina donacina L.
Mediterranean

Sunrise Tellin 3″
Tellina radiata L.
Fla. and West Indies
Abundant in sand

Virgate Tellin 2½″
Tellina virgata L.
Indo-Pacific; common

Full-blooded Tellin 3″
Tellina consanguinea Sby.
S. E. Asia; rare

Burnett's Tellidora 1½"
Tellidora burnetti Brod.
West Mexico; uncommon

Large Strigilla 1"
Strigilla carnaria L.
S.E. U.S.-Caribbean

Atlantic Grooved Macoma 3"
Psammotreta intastriata Say
Fla.-Caribbean

Bruguière's Macoma 2"
Macoma bruguièrei Hanl.
Philippines; uncommon

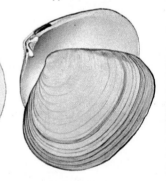

Close relatives of the true Tellins *(Tellina)* are the Strigillas of shallow, sandy bottoms. The shells are finely sculptured. The Macomas are twisted toward the back and the hinge lacks the lateral teeth.

SURF CLAMS (Mactridae) include many large edible clams with a spoon-shaped depression on the hinge. The Atlantic Surf Clam, common on sandy beaches, is the source of commercial clam chowder. The Duck Clams, *Labiosa,* of warm waters, have thin, fragile shells.

Oblong Surf Clam   5″
Lutraria oblonga Gmel.
Western Europe

Hians Surf Clam   3″
Mactra hians Philippi
S.E. Asia; common

Channeled Duck Clam   3″
Labiosa plicatella Lam.
Carolinas to Carib.; common

SANGUIN CLAMS (Garidae), of tropical, shallow, muddy waters, are closely related to the Tellin Shells. The thin, nearly transparent shells are drab in color with purple and browns predominating. About 100 species are known, many edible.

Violet Sanguin   2"
Soletellina violacea Lam.
East Indies; common

◄ **Nuttall's Mahogany Clam   3"**
Sanguinolaria nuttalli Conrad
Calif. to Mexico; common

Mediterranean Solecurtus   3"
Solecurtus strigilatus Linné
Mediterranean; uncommon

Operculate Sanguin   2"
Sanguinolaria cruenta Lightfoot
Caribbean-Brazil
Note that one valve is
flatter than the other.
Color often rose.

The **Gaudy Asaphis,** *Asaphis deflorata* L. shown above, is a colorful three-inch Sanguin Clam from the Caribbean. It is common in the intertidal zone in gravel. Colors may be rose, white or purple.

WEDGE CLAMS (Donacidae) are small, wedge-shaped clams found in the sand of nearly every temperate and tropical beach. Most of the 50 species are edible. The Atlantic Coquina is also known as the Butterfly Shell.

Atlantic Coquina   ½"
Donax variabilis Say
S.E. U.S.; makes good soup

Giant South African Wedge   3"
Donax serra Gmelin.
Republic of S. Africa
▼

Californian Wedge   1"
Donax californicus Conrad
Calif. to Panama

WEDGE CLAMS   **153**

JACKKNIFE CLAMS (Solenidae) are the true razor shells which dig a foot or more into sandy beaches with their curved, powerful foot. The Atlantic Jackknife is the largest and most common on the eastern Atlantic coast. It and Pacific species are harvested commercially. About 40 species are known. In the genus *Solen* the hinge teeth are at the very end of the shell; in *Ensis* they are a bit forward.

▲
Giant Japanese Solen 5″
Solen grandis Dkr.
Eastern Asia

Gould's Solen 5″
Solen gouldi Conrad
Eastern Asia ▼

Atlantic Jackknife Clam 6-7″
Ensis directus Conrad
Labrador-Carolinas ▼

Rose-spotted Solen 2″
Solen roseomaculatus Pils.
Japan

Philippi's Razor 2″
Ensiculus philippianus Dkr.
S.E. Asia; uncommon

SHIPWORMS (Teredinidae) are highly specialized mollusks. The adult is a destructive wood borer, honeycombing wooden ships and pilings with burrows cut by the small sharp-edged shells. The mantle secretes lime to line the tube, and two paddle-shaped pallets regulate the siphon openings. The Watering Pot (Clavagellidae) buries its shelly tube in the mud or sand. Lower end is perforated.

◀ **Watering Pot   5"**
Penicillus penis L.
Indo-Pacific

Common Shipworm   ½-2 ft.
Teredo navalis Linné ▶
Coastal N.A., Europe, Africa

shell valve   ½-1"

limy tube

pallet enlarged

early shells

pallets

siphon

open end

ARGONAUTS AND NAUTILUS, Class Cephalopoda, the most highly developed mollusks, also include the octopus and squid. Cephalopoda have heads with eight or more tentacles and highly developed eyes. The sexes are separate. All are carnivorous and most lack shells. The female Paper Nautilus secretes a shell with a specialized

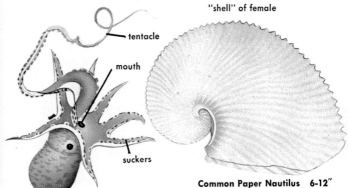

"shell" of female

tentacle

mouth

suckers

a male Argonaut

Common Paper Nautilus 6-12"
Argonauta argo Linné
World-wide, warm seas

Brown Paper Nautilus 3"
Argonauta hians Lightfoot
World-wide, warm seas

Nodose Paper Nautilus 5"
Argonauta nodosa Lightfoot
World-wide, warm seas

arm to protect her eggs. The smaller male makes no shell. The Chambered, or Pearly, Nautilus lives on ocean bottoms, crawling over the mud in search of crabs and shellfish. Surrounding the mouth are 60-90 small tentacles. The sealed-off, gas-filled chambers serve as a balancing apparatus. It is most abundant in the central Philippines.

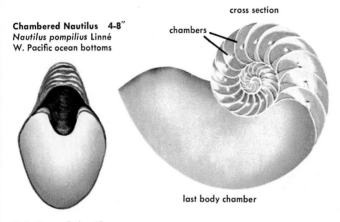

cross section

chambers

Chambered Nautilus 4-8"
Nautilus pompilius Linné
W. Pacific ocean bottoms

last body chamber

End views of the Chambered Nautilus. The female below is narrower than the male seen above.

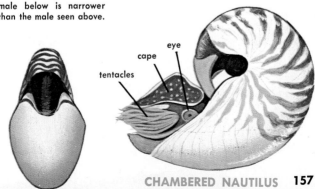

cape

eye

tentacles

INDEX

Because this book deals with 200 genera involving over 1100 scientific and popular species' names, this index has been condensed to aid the reader in locating the families and genera in which the illustrated species occur.

MEASURING SCALE (IN TOTHS OF AN INCH)

X Y